BLOWN TO BITS

20,000 FEET OVER PLOESTI

LEON COOPER

IUNIVERSE, INC.
BLOOMINGTON

Blown to Bits
20,000 Feet over Ploesti

The views expressed in this work are solely those of the author and do not necessarily reflect the views of the publisher, and the publisher hereby disclaims any responsibility for them.

iUniverse books may be ordered through booksellers or by contacting:

iUniverse
1663 Liberty Drive
Bloomington, IN 47403
www.iuniverse.com
1-800-Authors (1-800-288-4677)

Because of the dynamic nature of the Internet, any Web addresses or links contained in this book may have changed since publication and may no longer be valid.

ISBN: 978-1-4502-7040-3 (sc)
ISBN: 978-1-4502-7041-0 (dj)
ISBN: 978-1-4502-7042-7 (ebk)

Library of Congress Control Number: 2010916207

Printed in the United States of America

iUniverse rev. date: 3/1/2011

TABLE OF CONTENTS

ACKNOWLEDGEMENTS

I am profoundly indebted to those who contributed to the development of this book, without whose assistance it would have been virtually impossible. I am deeply honored for having had the opportunity to interact with family members of those who placed their lives on the line for America and its allies during World War II and am especially honored for the opportunities of having visited a few of these noble veterans who shared their stories, photos, and other memorabilia.

- Lt. Leo Bollei, pilot of the *Hearts and Flowers*
- Rick Bollei, major facilitator, son of Lt. Leo Bollei
- Jeanette (Seal) Keithley, daughter of Sgt. Wilburn Seal of the *Hearts and Flowers*
- Fred Seal, son of Sgt. Wilburn Seal
- Candy (Seal) Addison, major facilitator; cousin of both Sgt. Wilburn Seal, and Sgt. Wayne Simmons of the *Shilay-Lee*
- Nelda (Seal) Moran, sister of Sgt. Wayne Simmons, cousin of Sgt. Wilburn Seal, and classmate of the author
- Verna Lou Harris, widow of Sgt. Wayne Simmons
- Robert Wayne Simmons, son of Sgt. Wayne Simmons
- Gene Bluhm, son of Sgt. Robert Bluhm of the *Shilay-Lee*
- Sgt. Vernon MacNeil of the *Shilay-Lee*
- Maj. Stanley L. DeGeer, pilot of *Squeezie*, his wife, Eloise, and their adult children—Jan, David, Don, Ann

- Lt. Loring Cox, A-26 navigator/bombardier, technical resource
- Woody Crouch, son of Sgt. Raymond Crouch of the *Hearts and Flowers*
- Ronald K. Cooper, MD, technical resource
- Col. David Brookbank, Sr., Ret., U.S. Air Force pilot
- Ted Spitzmiller, writer and technical resource

TRIBUTE

This book is dedicated to the lives and memories of the *Greatest Americans*, those who sacrificed much—even their lives—that we might enjoy the freedom and opportunity to live in the greatest nation on the planet.

The men and women of the military—whether in war or in peace—stand at the threshold, fending off the wolves who would surely devour us. Except for these *Brave Americans*, we would not be standing here nor would we be speaking our chosen language.

We owe a tremendous debt of gratitude to these *Awesome Americans* who defended our freedom and preserved our liberty during World War II— a debt we can never fully repay. Without having walked in their shoes, one cannot truly understand or fully appreciate the sacrifices and hardships endured by these *Incredible Americans* and their families.

To Touch the Face of God

"Oh! I have slipped the surly bonds of Earth
And danced the skies on laughter-silvered wings;
Sunward I've climbed, and joined the tumbling mirth
Of sun-split clouds—and done a hundred things
You have not dreamed of—wheeled and soared and swung
High in the sunlit silence. Hov'ring there,
I've chased the shouting wind along, and flung
My eager craft through footless halls of air—
Up, up the long, delirious burning blue
I've topped the wind-swept heights with easy grace
Where never lark, or ever eagle flew—
And, while with silent, lifting mind I've trod
The high untrespassed sanctity of space,
Put out my hand, and touched the face of God."
—John Gillespie Magee, Jr.

During the desperate days of the Battle of Britain, hundreds of Americans enlisted in the Royal Canadian Air Force. Although contrary to the law—the Government was officially neutral—they volunteered to fight the Nazis.

John Gillespie Magee, Jr., was one of these Americans. He was eighteen years old when he enlisted and within the year was sent to England where he soon qualified to fly the Supermarine Spitfire fighter aircraft.

He rose to the rank of Pilot Officer while flying combat duties over France and England—against the German Luftwaffe.

On September 3, 1941, Magee flew a high altitude test flight in the latest model Spitfire-V. As he climbed past 30,000 feet, he was struck with the inspiration of a poem — *"To touch the face of God."*

On December 11, 1941—just three days after the U.S. entered the war, Pilot Officer John Gillespie Magee, Jr., was killed in a mid-air collision over England while descending through clouds. He was only nineteen years of age.

INTRODUCTION

I was nearing twelve years of age when, on December 7, 1941, the Japanese launched an unprovoked attack on Pearl Harbor, instantly thrusting the United States into World War II. Nearly four years later, the atomic bomb abruptly brought the war to an end with the unconditional surrender of Japan on September 2, 1945, a few months after Germany had surrendered in Europe.

One point must be made. During the six decades and three generations since World War II, there are some who look back over time and question why the United States dropped the atomic bomb on Japan. In interviews with more than fifty veterans of that war, none suggested that the atomic bomb should not have been dropped. Without exception, every one of them was grateful for the action taken and for not having to participate in the forthcoming invasion of Japan. It was projected by those in the field that an invasion would have drawn the war on for another six months or longer—at a cost of millions of lives, including many of America's finest.

This book describes what the war was like for twenty-four American aviators who carried the fight to the enemy in the horrific skies over Nazi-occupied Europe. A few made the ultimate sacrifice and were buried near where their blood was spilt. The majority of those imprisoned by the Germans was fortunate to have survived. Growing up through the Great Depression helped prepare these young men for the extreme hardships they would later encounter in the war.

EARLY FLYING EXPERIENCES

As a young lad, I was keenly interested in airplanes and flying. My parents were born around the time the Wright Brothers made history with man's first powered flight. Daddy and Mother risked life and limb by taking a flight in one of those early kite-like airplanes that barely stayed airborne. At the age of eight, they presented my brother and me with a ride in a big single-engine airplane making a cross-country tour. This brief experience was awesome, for it ignited a fire deep within my being, a flame that never waned. I learned to fly in a 65hp J-3 Piper Cub at the age of fifteen, earned a pilot license and owned a succession of airplanes later in life, always preferring an airplane to a nice automobile. After logging more than 3,800 pilot-hours and settling back to earth, the fire still glows. I'm still a pilot—I'll always be a pilot.

THE WARMONGERS

I was keenly aware of the war raging in Europe when we moved into the country west of Melrose, New Mexico, in 1938, where a battery powered radio brought the war directly into our simple little home. I recall to this day: "Good Morning, America. This is Edward R. Murrow reporting the latest from London, England …" It wasn't pretty. Adolph Hitler had risen from obscurity to become a hated monster, and the word "Nazi" had become synonymous with the highest forms of vulgarity in American speech. In my little mind—in my little world—I just knew that if someone handed me a rifle and sent me to Germany, I'd ferret out that perverted lunatic and blow him to bits! Obviously, I didn't quite grasp the complexity of the situation.

The German war machine was wreaking havoc in Europe by the time I'd reached the age of nine. The Nazis had overrun Poland, then the Netherlands. Cities were being obliterated and peoples crushed and annihilated in the quest to satisfy the fanatical ambitions of the German madman. Japan had begun the systematic takeover and destruction of China and its neighboring countries a few years earlier. Both super powers had developed warplanes and armament superior to anything the United States had to offer. Although the U.S. had developed a few warplanes prior to World War II, it had not kept pace with the axis warmongers.

Europe had become a raging inferno, with Germany waging unrelenting war against England, France and most of Europe. The United States remained neutral but was finally drawn into the global conflict following Japan's unprovoked attack on Pearl Harbor. The following day, Hitler declared war against America. Although German U-boats had already sunk dozens of American ships—with great loss of life and materiel—the United States had remained aloof. But, everything changed abruptly. Though two months shy of my twelfth birthday, I vividly recall those events and the years that followed.

Big changes came about almost overnight as the war effort shifted into high gear. Automobile manufacturing suddenly stopped in its tracks. Boeing, Douglas, Northrop, Consolidated, Lockheed, and others accelerated the development of bombers while Grumman, North American, Curtiss, Republic, and Bell developed fighter planes. The United States wasn't ready to fight a war, lagging far behind the advanced German and Japanese technologies. German Messerschmitt and Focke-Wulf fighter planes were highly maneuverable, with top speeds of over 350 mph. Japan's famed Zero fighter plane was highly maneuverable and could reach speeds in excess of 340 mph while our best fighter plane, the Curtiss P-40, topped out at around 325 mph. The British Spitfire, however, was among the best fighter planes at that time. Both the Germans and Japanese had twin-engine bombers with reasonable payloads and ranges—superior to anything in the U.S. arsenal. Several years after Germany and Japan launched deadly campaigns against their neighbors, the U.S. was still not prepared to wage a war.

The British Handley-Paige, Bristol, Sterling, and Lancaster bombers had ranges of up to 2,000 miles and bomb payloads of up to 10,000 lbs, but they were slow and effective only as daylight bombers. The German twin-engine Dornier and Heinkel bombers boasted the same range and less than half the payload, but they were fast, night-worthy and difficult to shoot down. The Japanese twin-engine Aichi and "Betty" bombers were near equals to those of the German planes.

On the flip side, however, the U.S. began in earnest, trying to catch up with the axis powers. England was at its knees, almost ready to buckle under the pressure of continuous nighttime bombardment by the Germans. Their factories could not keep pace with the demand for warplanes due to the intense bombing attacks. *Lend-lease* agreements were made whereby the U.S. supplied bombers and fighters for England to use in its defense, but these contributions added only about 5% to the British flying forces during the early years. Steady improvements in technology and performance resulted in new fighter craft that were almost as good as the German aircraft. Grumman developed and built the Wildcat fighter plane and, later, the Hellcat version, each designed to fly off the deck of an aircraft carrier. In the hands of a crack U.S. pilot, the Hellcat was far superior to the Japanese Zero fighter, achieving a kill ratio of almost twenty-to-one.

Numerous improvements were made to the experimental Boeing bomber, transforming it into the famous four-engine B-17 Flying Fortress. Though not fast—at around 200 mph—it was heavily armed, had a long range and could carry up to 8,000 lbs of bombs. A later bomber, the four-engine B-24, designed and built by Consolidated Aircraft, had a greater range and was faster but had a slightly smaller payload.

Soon, several high performance fighter planes were rolling off the assembly lines in the U.S.—the Lockheed P-38 Lightning, Republic P-47 Thunderbolt, North American P-51 Mustang, Vought/Sikorsky F4U Corsair and Grumman F6F Hellcat—which in the long run signaled doom for the enemy aviators.

THE NEW REPLACES THE OLD

As the war intensified in Europe, so too did my quest to fly. My father fashioned toy airplanes from wood scraps salvaged from apple crates, complete with propellers that spun in the never-ending breezes of eastern New Mexico. My first attempt at real flying was unsuccessful, having been inspired by the comic character, "Wimpy," in the "Popeye" comic strip of the Sunday newspaper. Wimpy attached wings to his arms and flew to safety from a sinking ship. If Wimpy, an overweight, rotund character, could fly like that, I could surely do so.

I cut 'wings' from a large piece of cardboard, attached them to my arms with heavy twine, climbed a ladder, poised on the edge of the roof and spread my wings in flight. I don't recall how high I ascended or the distance covered, because gravity abruptly gained the upper hand—I only recall being in pain, lying on my back, looking upward toward the sky and seeing stars in mid-day! Luckily, no broken bones, but my confidence was severely shattered. A lot was gained from that experience.

By the age of ten, the box-shaped airplanes that infrequently passed over Melrose were being replaced by ever increasing numbers of military aircraft on training missions. Our community was far removed from large populated areas and industrial centers, and the region boasted better flying conditions than most other parts of the country. For this reason, numerous training bases were established nearby for several types of military aircraft. Before long, P-40 fighters, B-24 bombers, Cessna and Stearman trainers, gliders towed by DC-3 transport planes—were everyday sights. It's no wonder I became caught up in the excitement of advancing aviation technology.

As a never-before-observed airplane made an appearance overhead, I decided that I'd become a pilot of that particular aircraft. Whenever a different one appeared, I changed my mind and decided on another. My wild imagination had no limit!

THE GREAT DEPRESSION

The American military consisted of young men who grew up during the Great Depression. In reality, it was perhaps the greatest gift of which one could have dreamed, for the youth learned important life lessons through everyday experiences under the tutelage of superb role models—fathers and mothers, aunts and uncles, grandparents, cousins, friends, neighbors.

People were happy, not being fettered by the accumulation of things they didn't really need. Everyone knew his or her neighbor and often depended on that individual for one thing or another. Mrs. Kemper would come over to borrow a cup of flour, and Mother would send her home with "two". Mrs. Farrar would go over to Mrs. Kemper's house to borrow three eggs but would come home with "six". Mother would cross the street to borrow a cup of sugar from Mrs. Farrar and would come home with "two". No one kept account of "who owed who what." These three ladies—true saints having different religious preferences—never once discussed the merits or differences in each but, rather, recognized the common goals and principles. Neither did conversations revolve around personal views on politics or religion. People worked together for the better good of all.

Crime was uncommon but, when a crime was committed, the offender expected to be punished accordingly. Neither the ACLU nor a high-powered attorney was present to contort the law in order to get special treatment for one who committed a crime. Neither could money buy a "not guilty" verdict for one who was obviously culpable.

The large majority of Americans held to the higher moral ground, abiding by the principles laid out by the forefathers of this great country. People accepted responsibility.

YOUTHS STEP FORWARD

It's no wonder that young Americans came forward to fight for the lives and freedom of other Americans. It wasn't for money or fame. They did it out of love, respect and responsibility. During the late 1930s, when most families were in dire straits from the fallout of the long and arduous Great Depression, young men often joined the military in order to earn twenty dollars a month, sending most of it back home to help their families. This wasn't uncommon; it was ordinary. The military forces were made up of these volunteers who came up through the Great Depression.

In late 1941, American military personnel were scattered across the country—others were serving in Panama, the Philippines, or another distant place. More than two thousand were killed during the aerial firestorm on that fateful December day in 1941 when America was startled from its complacency and suddenly thrust into war, one we were ill prepared to undertake. The entire world was in peril.

Overnight, young people stepped forward to enlist in the military, many of them not yet out of high school. Military training facilities sprang up all over the country for the purpose of training recruits for the Army, Navy, Marines and Air Corps. Troop demand increased to the point that the government established a draft system whereby recruits were inducted into service according to age and qualification. Every male age 18–35 was required to register for the draft and was classified as "1-A". High school students eighteen years of age and older were usually given deferments until after graduating. Those working at strategic jobs were given deferments of up to a year after which their status was re-evaluated. For the most part, young men between the ages of eighteen and twenty-five were called up first, followed by those twenty-five years of age and older. Those few inductees who failed physical or mental examinations were sent home and re-classified as "4-F".

Many young men opted to join the Navy, Marines or Army Air Corps (later, the Army Air Force) rather than waiting to be selected by the draft. Whenever an individual enlisted in the Army Air Corps—hoping to become a pilot—he was required to pass both physical and academic tests in order to qualify for Aviation Cadet School. If he failed one or the other, he was described as having "washed out" and was transferred to another track (i.e., navigator or bombardier school, flight engineer school, gunnery or radio school). Those who had already completed one or two years of college were more likely to be accepted into the Aviation Cadet program.

WHY COMPILE THIS STORY?

I was genuinely motivated to collect and assemble the inter-related accounts comprising this story due to my admiration for—and association with—those who fought in World War II. Most came back after the war, but many didn't. The following are but a few with whom I was personally acquainted.

Alva Simmons, Glendell Monk, Lee Roach, W. A. Noffsgar, and Robert Coffey were stationed in the Philippines, overrun by the Japanese, forced onto the *Bataan Death March* and relegated to slave labor in Japan's salt and coal mines. Glen and Alva survived most of the war as prisoners but never made it back. Jack Love didn't make it back from the war in Europe; neither did his brother, Dan Love, just two grades ahead of me. Dan was killed on the deck of an aircraft carrier in the Pacific. He lied about his age in order to join the fight for his country; he was only seventeen years old—the ultimate patriot.

I was a visitor at the Kemper home on June 4, 1944, when Mr. Vester Lea delivered a telegram with the tragic news that Kempers' eldest son had been killed during heavy fighting to secure Anzio Beach Head in Italy. Captain Emory "Andrew" Kemper had grown up directly across the street from my home. A few days later—on June 17—the C. B. Myers family learned that *their* son, Captain Harold Myers, had perished in China. His B-29 Super Fortress crashed into a mountainside following a bombing raid on Japan. Both Harold and Andrew lived very near me—just a block apart. Luther "Sonny" Hines died in England on March 13, 1945, near the end of the war in Europe, in a mid-air collision involving his P-51 Mustang after mixing it up with enemy fighters in the skies over Germany. Harold Glenn and Leo Daley went down with their ship, the *Lexington*, during heavy fighting in the Pacific. Others died in foxholes, in prison camps or other places far from home. These stories were repeated again and again throughout the war as families and friends mourned the losses of young men we knew so very well—who had died so young. They were our schoolmates, neighbors, friends—and then, they were gone.

Other local warriors included Fred Highley, Air Force test pilot; Polk Follis, who survived fifty missions over Germany as a tail turret gunner on a B-17 bomber; Travis Hoover, who piloted the second B-25 to fly off the deck of the U.S.S. Hornet during the first aerial assault on the Japanese mainland in a thousand years—on April 18, 1942; Robert Widner, who served in Iceland and returned to finish high school with my class; Leo Robinson, who was on his way to the Pacific when the Japanese surrendered; and David Shoup, who lost a leg in the war but returned as my biology teacher in the fall of 1945—he continued to wear his uniform to school, with pride.

Amado Lucero, a country boy from central New Mexico, is buried not far from where he gave his life near Rome, Italy, in late 1944. His sister, Filia Perea, vividly remembers the last time she saw him sixty-six years ago as he headed off to war. Amado—and other young men like him—are sorely missed, leaving a void that remains to this day. Others came back physically whole but not emotionally the same, for they'd left as young kids just like me but returned as mature young men harboring unpleasant memories locked in the backs of their minds—memories far too painful to share with others.

As the youngest student entering Southern Nazarene University in 1946, I was privileged to be among hundreds of veterans returning from World War II—they'd fought in the *Battle of the Bulge,* the *Invasion of Okinawa*, the *Deserts of Africa*, the *Skies over Europe*, the *Normandy Invasion*. One of those, Captain Earl Wassom, was back in school a month after dropping bombs on Berlin! These were my mentors. At Los Alamos, I was honored to be on the staff with more than a dozen veteran pilots, navigators, bombardiers and aircraft gunners—and with

Marines who survived the *Invasion of Iwo Jima*, soldiers who fought on the ground from one foxhole to another, and with Navy and Infantry men who were part of the *Normandy Invasion*.

It is not only for those who died, but for those who returned, that I'm inspired, ever driven, to record as many of their stories as possible. Few World War II veterans remain today. They are rapidly disappearing. Let us dedicate ourselves to preserving *their* stories before they become forever lost in the mist of time.

This is *Their Story*.

TIMELINES

DECEMBER 7, 1941

On a bright, sunny Sunday afternoon, a handful of happy lads played softball on a sandy lot across the street from my cousins' home in Portales, New Mexico. The Great Depression was still dragging on as two dozen family members—aunts and uncles, cousins, nieces and nephews, fathers and mothers—gathered for a Sunday afternoon visit. At around 2 PM, a neighbor, Bill Simms, hurried past our ball game, stopped momentarily and held up a tabloid-size newspaper with the bold headlines: *"U.S. IN WAR!"* The tranquil atmosphere was shattered in the blink of an eye! *"This can't be true!"* I told myself. My cousins—Leo and Boots Robinson—and the other kids were equally stunned. Mr. Simms rushed over to the house with the dreadful news. The adults huddled around the radio in the cramped living room, as Uncle Winfred tuned in a station. We children considered what was to come.

December 7, 1941; Somber faces in this photo taken shortly after the news of the Japanese attack on Pearl Harbor; *front row, L to R*: Leon Cooper, Boots Robinson, Leo Robinson, Ronald Cooper

The Japanese had launched a sneak attack on Pearl Harbor, sinking ships and killing thousands of innocent people in one of the most dastardly military actions the world had ever known. Their military forces had been warring against China since 1931, before launching a full-scale invasion in mid-1937—burning villages, destroying crops, and committing unspeakable atrocities against the people.

Although I was not quite twelve at the time, I still recall those events as though they occurred yesterday. More than sixty young men from our small community of Melrose, New Mexico, marched off to war. Some were still in high school. Of the two dozen who didn't come home from the war, most were buried where their blood spilled at some faraway place. I knew every one of these courageous men. They were my neighbors, upper schoolmates, cousins and friends. They attended our churches, walked our paths, were in my scout troop; we worked, rode bicycles, and played together. A part of each is forever instilled in my being.

Words are not sufficient to honor those who placed their lives in harm's way for each of us—living in peril every day, every hour, every moment—bravely facing a ferocious, destructive enemy. Their dedication and heroism was beyond measure. This book provides the reader with an accurate account of the personal experiences of twenty-four courageous Americans whose lives became intertwined in the hellacious skies over Ploesti, Rumania, during World War II.

MAY 5, 1944

14:30 hrs: *BAM!* The *Shilay-Lee* shuddered from the concussion of an 88-millimeter shell that exploded below and off to the left, rocking the huge aircraft off center! Lt. Julius Altvater, his eyes intently focused into the view scope of the Norden bombsight, toggled the control lever to the left and to the right, attempting to keep the heavy bomber on track toward today's target—the huge oil refining complex just outside Ploesti, Rumania. Lt. Robert Boyle had switched control of the ship to Altvater three minutes earlier as they approached the I.P.—the initial point of the bomb run. *BAM! BAM!* Other shells exploded nearby. The German gunners were accurate on this day, having set the barometric fuses so their shells would detonate at the same elevation at which the main body of the formation was flying. Bursts of black smoke were everywhere, indicating where shells exploded, scattering thousands of razor-sharp steel shards—"flak"—into the path of the oncoming bombers.

14:31 hrs: *BAM!* The *Shilay-Lee* lurched like a bobsled bounding over a hard bump. *CRACK! PING! PING!* Metal shards pierced the aircraft's wings, one piece slicing into the right inboard engine, knocking it out of commission. Boyle quickly feathered the propeller in order to reduce drag. The noise of air rushing through broken panes in the plastic nose was nothing new to Altvater; he kept his eyes glued to the view scope as the target zone approached the cross-hairs in the bombsight.

14:32 hrs: *CRASH!* A piece of shrapnel ripped through the Plexiglas nose, instantly destroying Lt. Robert Barker's navigational instruments. He rushed forward, jerked the nose turret doors open and yelled to Sgt. Wayne Simmons, asking whether he wanted his parachute. Barker figured there was a good possibility they might have to abandon the aircraft. Simmons nodded his head *"No"* and pointed his gloved hand forward, indicating that he'd remain in the turret. Simmons closed the turret doors and scanned the sky for enemy fighters. It was scary. It seemed like a hundred shells were exploding every second, some so close that they rocked the ship, causing it to lurch and shudder. Puffballs of black smoke and invisible flak were everywhere, so dense that it appeared as though one could walk on it!

The oil refinery, now a raging inferno, was sending up huge, columns of black smoke that rose higher than the bombers.

14:33 hrs: *BOOM!* The *Shilay-Lee* convulsed violently but continued to fly. The plane's intercom system went suddenly dead. They had suffered a direct hit from an 88-millimeter shell!

14:34 hrs: Simmons glanced to his right and noticed the inboard propeller had stopped rotating—the number-three engine was dead! The number-four engine was belching smoke but otherwise operating, and the right landing gear was dangling below. He was concerned but not overly worried, because he'd experienced rough situations on previous missions. The plane was still flying with the remaining three engines running at full throttle. For the moment, they were keeping up with other bombers in the formation.

Sgt. Vernon MacNeil retracted the ball turret to find himself in a vicious firestorm! A shell had penetrated the forward midsection and exploded, sending metal shards in all directions. Sgt Robert Bluhm lay on the floor near his waist gunner position—blood oozing from under his flight helmet! He was not exactly conscious and appeared unaware of what was going on. A piece of shrapnel had penetrated the front of his helmet and helmet liner, punctured his insulated flight cap and knocked him daffy. The sound of rushing air was deafening, whooshing through dozens of gaping holes in the fuselage. Visibility was difficult, and heat from the fire was searing. MacNeil grabbed a fire extinguisher and tried to put out the flames as Cpl. Douglas Millar, a photographer who happened to be onboard, attended Bluhm.

14:35 hrs: Heavy smoke and thick ground haze caused by bombs from other aircraft made the target difficult to identify with high certainty but, when the cross-hairs in the bombsight passed directly over the A.P.—the aiming point, or presumed target in this case—Altvater pressed the bomb release—*"BOMBS AWAY!"* He yelled.

He rose to find a gaping hole in the forward nose and air rushing by at hurricane force. He wondered aloud—*"Where's Barker? Had he been blown out of the plane?"*

14:36 hrs: Altvater rushed toward the flight deck, having to crawl around the nose wheel housing and other obstacles.

14:38 hrs: Altvater found Barker holding Copilot Sam Moore's body back off the control column and Pilot Boyle trying to fly the *Shilay-Lee* with his left arm—his right arm and shoulder had been hit by shrapnel from the explosion—he was bleeding and in bad shape. Boyle yelled for Altvater to help Barker pull Moore out of the copilot seat—but, his bulky flight suit and the confined space made it impossible to pull him out.

14:40 hrs: Sgt. James Benardini, top turret gunner and flight engineer, dropped down from the turret and helped extricate Moore; they laid him on the floor. Benardini immediately set about assisting Boyle in dealing with the seriously disrupted systems—engines, propellers, fuel, electrical, hydraulics…

14:42 hrs: MacNeil made his way up the catwalk, having to contend with slippery footing from hydraulic oil that had sprayed over everything. Arriving at the flight deck, he found Lt. Sam Moore lying on the floor, a jagged metal shard protruding from the back of his neck. Boyle was flying the badly crippled ship with his left arm, and Barker was in the copilot seat assisting him in keeping the *Shilay-Lee* in level attitude and on course with the rest of the bomber group.

14:43 hrs: MacNeil informed Boyle of a bad fire back in the midsection. Boyle didn't reply—he was much too preoccupied with simply trying to keep the plane airborne.

14:45 hours: Altvater and MacNeil took up the fire fighting chore. The situation appeared hopeless, flames having engulfed the oxygen tanks that were now feeding the flames!

14:48 hrs: The fire crept ever closer to the left-side fuel tank located near the wing root attachment. Aluminum components were beginning to melt—it was obvious that the *Shilay-Lee* was about finished. Realizing the futility of their efforts—wind scattering the spray in all directions, much of it back into their faces—and with the heat being intolerable, Altvater rushed to the flight deck and informed Boyle that it was a losing battle! The *Shilay-Lee* was beyond hope, and the end was near—VERY near!

14:49 hrs: With the situation extremely grave—the plane would surely blow up at any moment—Boyle asked Barker how far it was to Yugoslavia, hoping he could nurse the mortally damaged ship back over neutral territory. Structural parts were beginning to fail from the searing heat produced by the unstoppable monster blowtorch. There wasn't enough time—it was too risky! Boyle nodded for them to get out as he wrestled to hold the *Shilay-Lee* in level attitude.

14:51 hrs: Altvater fought his way back through the flames and yelled at his nearby mates—Sgt. Hugh Moore, the tail gunner; Sgt. Allen Christianson, the left waist gunner, and Millar and MacNeil! *"Get outa here fast—NOW!*

14:52 hrs: MacNeil and Millar disconnected Bluhm's electrical and oxygen lines, rolled him over, checked his parachute harness, and dragged him to the open bombay. In his semi-conscious state, Bluhm was unable to comprehend the situation. He resisted their efforts and had to be forcefully persuaded. They shoved him out—head first.

14:55 hrs: Millar bailed out, followed by Christianson.

14:57 hrs: Moore bailed out, followed by MacNeil.

15:01 hrs: *"Where's Simmons???"* Altvater wasted not a second! He rushed forward as quickly as he could—fighting his way back through the fire, climbing over obstacles, weaseling around the nose wheel housing, finally arriving at the forward nose. Simmons, unaware of what was going on back in the mid-section, was startled by the turret doors suddenly being jerked open—It was Altvater.
　"Hey! Let's get outa here—Fast!"
　A German FW-190 fighter plane appeared from underneath, just as Simmons turned. The enemy pilot, seeing that the *Shilay-Lee* was mortally wounded, held his fire and waved at Simmons. Simmons lowered his guns, returned the wave and leaped from the turret.

Grabbing his parachute, he followed Altvater rearward. They pushed their chutes ahead while crawling around the nose gear housing and through the tight passageway.

15:05 hrs: Arriving at the flight deck, Simmons observed Lt. Sam Moore's body lying on the floor. He was dead—probably killed instantly. He noted Boyle having a badly injured right arm and bloody shoulder but otherwise managing to fly the fatally crippled ship pretty well.

"*Where's the rest of the crew?*" He puzzled! There wasn't a second to think about it!

15:07 hrs: "*Get outa here before she blows!*" Altvater yelled!

15:08 hrs: Simmons attached the snaps to his parachute and made his way to the bombay. What he observed was beyond description—the entire midsection was engulfed in flames, with angry tongues of fire leaping from the floor to the ceiling!

15:10 hrs: He took one look and, without hesitation, leaped through the open bombay and disappeared below.

15:11 hrs: After free-falling for several seconds, he pulled the ripcord; his parachute blossomed and gave a gentle tug as it caught air at around 16,000 feet. He felt as though he were hanging in the sky, not falling. It was suddenly peaceful—eerily quiet for a few seconds—until the silence was interrupted by an explosion off to the west. It was the *Shilay-Lee!* His heart sank, assuming the rest of the crew had been blown to bits. To his relief, he looked up and spotted two parachutes between himself and the broken ship, gently floating earthward. He watched the *Shilay-Lee,* now separated into two parts, the larger front section still headed west as though in flight until plowing into the Rumanian countryside not far away.

A lifetime of events had transpired in little over half an hour.

The frigid cold at 20,000 feet was replaced by the late spring warmth in the skies above the countryside northwest of Craiova, Rumania, as the ground started racing up toward Simmons. To the west, other parachutes floated gently downward as the 'friendly appearing' landscape rapidly rushed up to meet them. What fate awaited these American 'intruders,' once their feet touched down on this foreign, unfriendly soil?

THIRTEEN DAYS LATER—MAY 18, 1944

10:32 hrs: German FW-190s and Me-109s suddenly came out of nowhere, attacking from the rear, sweeping diagonally across the top of the formation from left to the right and promptly disappearing back into the clouds. The 80% cloud cover allowed them to play 'cat-and-mouse' games with the bombers. They wondered, *"Where are those dreaded P-51 fighter escorts? Are they waiting above, to come out of hiding and rip us to pieces?"* The harassment continued off and on for the next several minutes, with several bombers getting badly raked. Unaware that there were no escorts on this day, the German pilots were playing it cautiously.

10:47 hrs: Sgt. Jack Haney walked along the narrow catwalk, arming the 500-lb bombs by removing the safety pins from the nose vanes. A quick check confirmed that all was in order and that the bombs should drop properly—the spinner on the nose of each bomb would 'unscrew' in the airstream several seconds after falling earthward, thus freeing the inertial plunger that would detonate the bomb upon impact with the ground. The pilot, Lt. Leo Bollei, activated the switch that opened the bombay doors, once Haney had returned to his tail gunner position and advised Bollei.

10:48 hrs: Enemy fighter planes were now attacking from every angle. Sgt. Leslie Jensen rolled his 44-inch ball turret to the right and peered directly between his knees—the only decent field of vision from the turret—looking straight down the middle of the twin 50-calibre Brownings. *"One…two…three…four."* Four parachutes blossomed from a B-24 Liberator trailing fire as it went into a slow, descending turn back under the *Hearts and Flowers*. Jensen spun the ball turret back to the left in time to line his sights on a trio of Me-109s veering to avoid collision with a B-17 they'd attacked. He fired off a quick burst—*"TAT-TAT-TAT-TAT!"* A puff of smoke, and the fighter on the right literally exploded in the blink of an eye! *"Got him!"* Turning back, he counted: *"Five…six…seven…eight. Where are those other two?"* The wounded B-24 was a goner. Perhaps he'd missed seeing the ninth and tenth parachutes.

It was lonesome in the ball turret except for the plane's intercom system through which Jensen communicated with the pilot and crew. It was especially worrisome on this day, because 150 bombers had been called back to base because of deteriorating weather. Sixty-four other bombers continued on, either because they didn't hear the radio message to turn back, or they ignored it. Worse still, the fighter escorts had also returned to base, not realizing some of the bombers were proceeding without escort protection.

Jensen had the best seat in the house for observing everything below the plane. Unfortunately, he was witness to a B-24 going down and a couple of B-17s getting badly shot up. He noticed two other bombers trailing smoke but apparently not in really bad shape at the moment. Fortresses often returned to base trailing smoke and having gaping holes and missing pieces.

10:50 hrs: *"Bombardier to pilot! Crossing the I.P!"*

"Roger, it's yours!" Lt. Leo Bollei monitored the instrument panel as Lt. Keith Winder took control of the aircraft for the next few minutes. The enemy fighters were suddenly gone, but big problems loomed ahead. Hundreds of black puff-balls of smoke indicated the German gunners had been fairly accurate in setting the fuses so their shells would explode very near the elevation of the incoming bombers.

10:52 hrs: *"Another Fortress took a hit!"* Jensen followed the wounded plane as it began to lose altitude, counting seven open parachutes before losing sight of the aircraft.

10:54 hrs: The B-17 next to the *Hearts and Flowers* was flying on three engines, with the propeller feathered on the number-one engine. Although it was holding position in the formation, the left wing was noticeably higher than the right one.

Lt. Winder followed the path of the *Hearts and Flowers* through the view scope on the bombsight, watching as the cross-hairs crept ever closer to the A.P.—the aiming point.

And, here it came! *"BOOM! BOOM!"* Shells were exploding directly ahead! *"CRACK! PING! CRASH!"* The *Hearts and Flowers* was taking hits from "flak"—razor-sharp metal shards, or shrapnel, resulting from the exploding shells. The big bomber lurched each time a shell exploded nearby, but Winder toggled the control lever left or right, managing to keep the plane on track toward the A.P.

10:55 hrs: *"About a minute to go!"* Winder advised Bollei.
"*Roger!*" Bollei replied.

10:56 hrs: *"BOMBS AWAY!"* Winder yelled. The aircraft rose abruptly as 8,000 lbs of bombs dropped away and accelerated toward the A.P.—the presumed target for the mission. Bollei took control of the *Hearts and Flowers* as they started a gentle right turn off the target to set up the homeward course.

10:57 hrs: *"What's our heading for home, Karlovitz?"* Bollei inquired of the navigator.
"*Go for two-fifty degrees magnetic, when you can.*" Lt. William Karlovitz was an excellent navigator and understood well that the bombers would regroup and move into tight formation as quickly as possible. Bollei needed to know the desired heading in case they became separated from the other bombers.

But, now there was a big problem! The bombbay doors refused to close! They were hanging down into the slipstream, creating tremendous drag! Evidently, they'd been shot up or damaged from flak. Someone, probably the engineer—Sgt. Wilburn Seal—tried kicking them loose so they could be retracted, but it was useless. The drag was terrible.

Bollei powered up the engines, trying to keep up with the pack. They'd been operating at 85% power, but he didn't dare allow the plane to lag behind lest they'd become a prime target for enemy fighters. At full throttle, he was barely able to overcome the extra drag, but the added stress greatly increased the risk of engine failure. He certainly couldn't maintain full throttle for long, but perhaps they could get closer to friendly territory before throttling back.

And, here they came—again! Me-109 and FW-190 enemy fighters arriving in full force! There were at least 150 of them, perhaps as many as 200! They came in like a waterfall—a dozen abreast—pouring lead to the bombers!

In came a string of fighters, just like ducks heading down toward water! *"TAT! TAT! TAT!"* Seal fired a short burst from his top turret position. The lead Me-109 never knew what hit him as his aircraft exploded in a flash! *"Got him!"* He was right on target—just like leading ducks in flight! Two more enemy fighters came in too close, and Seal sent them down trailing smoke. *"Head shots!"*

Jensen poured slugs into another that peeled down through the bombers, sending it away trailing dense black smoke. Sgt. Raymond Crouch fired off bursts from his left-waist gunner position, slicing a piece of rudder off a FW-190. Sgt. Joseph Cutrone put another FW-190 out of action from the right waist position.

10:59 hrs: The past two minutes seemed like a lifetime, as the enemy came in—a dozen or more at a time—like 'walls of blazing lightning!' So many of them were lined up at times that they provided perfect targets for Bollei's shooters! Sgt. Jack Haney got direct hits into two enemy fighters zipping past his position at the tail.

11:00 hrs: *"LIEUTENANT! THE 'NUMBER-THREE' IS ON FIRE!"* Neither Bollei nor Flight Officer Sydney Fisher could see the flames curling from below the inboard engine on the right side, but Jensen had a bird's eye view, and the flames were trailing just a few feet from the ball turret!

A group of P-38 Lightnings suddenly appeared and chased the enemy fighters away but, for the *Hearts and Flowers*, it was too late. Bollei recognized the futility of their situation—the *Hearts and Flowers* would explode into a gigantic fireball the moment the fire reached the right-side wing tank—and it was getting close! Dangerously close! Realizing he was in no position to make ten dead heroes out of his crew and, with no time to waste, he yelled over the intercom: *"Everybody out! We're going to blow up any moment! Check your chutes! GET OUT— NOW!—FAST!*

The men knew exactly what to do. They were prepared for such emergencies. They rushed toward the open bombay.

11:01 hrs: Cutrone and Winder jumped, followed in quick succession by, Karlovitz, Jensen, Haney, Seal, Fisher, and Sgt. Edward Buffington.

11:04 hrs: Crouch suddenly turned to run back into the fuselage; Bollei shouted at him, *"Crouch! What are you thinking!"* Crouch was gone only a few seconds before reappearing; he'd left an insulated glove at his waist gunner station. He dove through the open bombay and disappeared below.

11:06 hrs: Bollei leveled the doomed aircraft as best he could, checked his parachute harness, disconnected his oxygen and intercom lines, popped the hatch opening and jumped out head first. The frigid air at 22,000 feet swirled viciously around him as he tumbled down through space for what seemed like a long time.

11:08 hrs; He pulled the ripcord. His parachute blossomed and then jerked sharply as it caught air at 17,000 feet. It was suddenly quiet—very quiet—like a twilight zone! He was grateful that everyone had gotten out of the mortally wounded aircraft safely.

11:09 hrs: Lt. Leo Bollei, pilot of the *Hearts and Flowers,* had but a few minutes to ponder the situation as he drifted downward toward unfriendly territory and an uncertain future.

Fast forward about sixty years, to January, 2004—to the home of Stanley and Eloise DeGeer in Albuquerque, New Mexico, where they're hosting a Super Bowl Sunday gathering. Stan ushers the author into his 'office' where an artist's painting of a P-51 Mustang fighter plane adorns the wall. *"Number 79, 'Squeezie.' That's my bird! Come back later, when there's not a party goin' on, and I'll share some things with you."* Although the author had known Stanley DeGeer as a good friend for over fifty years, the only thing he'd ever mentioned about his involvement in World War II was that he 'flew a Mustang in the Air Force.' A week later, the *"Stanley DeGeer Story"* began to unfold as he described being based in Italy and flying escort for B-17 and B-24 bombers carrying out missions over German-occupied Europe.

Fast forward again—to February, 2007—to the home of Candy Seal Addison in Lubbock, Texas. Seated around the dining table are Candy, Jeanette Seal Keithley, and Nelda Seal Moran—first cousins— and myself, delving into a long past chapter in their lives. They're further connected by the events of World War II during which Jeanette's father and Nelda's brother—one in a B-17 Flying Fortress and the other in a B-24 Liberator—were blown out of the skies over Ploesti, Rumania, in some of the most horrific and brutal firestorms the world has ever known. By some miracle, both men survived the war but shared the painful parts of their stories with few.

Fast forward a few months to December, 2007, to the Bollei home in Michigan where Leo Bollei, his wife Elizabeth, and son Rick, take me on an awesome journey back in time—to the deadly skies over Europe—where dodging bullets was an everyday routine of life and death.

Step ahead a few months—to the spring of 2008 and through the following year— when Vernon MacNeil shares his memories, many of them unpleasant, including his account of being blown out of the skies over Rumania in 1944.

Then, out of the blue—miracles! Just when it seemed nothing more would be forthcoming—Gene Bluhm, Robert Wayne Simmons and his mother, Verna Lou Harris, are located—alive and well! Many missing parts of this large 'jigsaw puzzle' quickly came together to provide a well defined picture of what happened in the deadly skies over Ploesti, Rumania in 1944.

Here, for the first time, are the intertwined accounts of twenty-four of America's finest who answered their country's call during World War II. This book is only part of their story, for the whole story would consume a ton of paper bound into a hundred volumes. Find a comfortable chair, relax, and travel with us back to another time—to another place—when things were not quite the same as they are today.

WAR COMES TO AMERICA!

The Japanese assault on Pearl Harbor "awakened a sleeping giant," as predicted by Admiral Yamamoto of the Japanese Imperial Navy. America seemed to come to life after having struggled through the decade of the Great Depression. We were at war! Americans everywhere took up the cause, turning their undivided attention to the task at hand—joining our allies in defeating those who would otherwise take the lands and enslave decent peoples around the globe. It wasn't going to be easy. Americans would tighten their belts and contribute to the united effort in every way possible in order to defeat tyranny, to protect our freedom and way of life—at any cost.

The ranks of the military swelled enormously—almost overnight—as young men lined up to enlist. School kids worked on farms and in businesses in place of those who'd marched off to war. The government set up regulatory boards for the purpose of conserving resources and achieving the best possible efficiency. Essential items were rationed, including motor fuel, certain foodstuffs and other materials required by the military. Scrap metals and rubber were collected for reprocessing into military hardware. People bought war bonds in support of the war effort. Everywhere, people sacrificed, scrimped and saved.

The consumption of imported materials—sugar, coffee, rubber, bananas and fruits—was sharply curtailed as Nazi U-boats cruised about the Atlantic Ocean, sinking any vessel not flagged as friendly to their cause. Commercial and passenger ships were sent to the bottom of the sea with incredible loss of life and material.

Passenger train movement increased dramatically as thousands upon thousands of soldiers were transported across the country. Before long, mile-long freight trains loaded with army tanks, cannons, personnel carriers and crated hardware of every kind—engines, tires, barrels, trailers, materiel—sped from one horizon to the other as mobilization moved into high gear.

We moved to the country west of Melrose in 1938. The nearest airport, *Portair*, was located next to the village of Blacktower, seventeen miles east of our village. It sat along the AT&SF Railroad line that passed through Melrose. *Portair* became *Clovis Airport* briefly and then *Clovis Army Air Base*. The runways were widened and extended in preparation for squadrons of B-24 bombers that began arriving in 1942. Hangars and other facilities were rapidly constructed as bomber training exercises began in earnest. The base was renamed *Cannon Air Force Base* a couple of years later.

A smaller aerial training base was established at Fort Sumner, thirty-seven miles west of Melrose. Several squadrons of P-40 Flying Tiger fighter planes and other aircraft, including Stearman biplanes and twin-engine Cessna plywood-and-fabric trainer aircraft, arrived shortly. About twenty-five miles northwest of Melrose, an isolated airstrip was constructed for a contingent of thirty gliders and a couple dozen C-47 tow planes. Observer planes and other miscellaneous craft were located at each site. More than a hundred airplanes were stationed within a 40-mile radius of our community.

Radio navigation was still rather primitive—navigational training involved the use of altimeters, compasses, landmarks and standard broadcast radio signals. A major navigational tool was the railroad. Airplanes consistently flew along major railroads from one point to another. Our home sat a hundred yards from the AT&SF railroad tracks, so we experienced a lot of air traffic. This was totally delightful to a young lad.

In addition, the bombing practice range was less than three miles southwest of our house. Small groups of B-24 bombers—in a string— would approach from the east, at low level, following large, numbered, white A-frame structures spaced every mile along the railroad tracks.

They flew directly over our house, westbound, causing it to shudder, made a sweeping turn back toward the north and climbed to an altitude of perhaps 4,000 feet. A few minutes later, they circled back southward in a tight box formation and passed directly over the bombing range to drop 100-pound practice bombs.

The targets at the bombing range consisted of large forms laid out with caliche material (white clay) configured like aircraft carriers, destroyers, and battleships. During each run, a plane would drop a dozen or so bombs that fell in a zigzag pattern. These practice bombs were about four feet in length by nine inches in diameter—filled with sand. A small explosive charge (in the form of an oversized shotgun shell) was located in the tailpiece along with a small bag of white powder. At the moment of impact, a spring-retained inertial plunger struck the primer cap, causing the charge to explode, producing an instantaneous white cloud that served as a photo marker for observers in the formation. A group of planes might make three or four passes before expending its bombs and returning to the base.

The glider exercises were exciting. Twin-engine C-47 airplanes towed two gliders each, in a "V" formation, with one glider trailing off to the left and high and the other glider off to the right and low. They would pass over our house at such low elevation that one could have struck the tow plane with a rock. Rivets could be counted, and facial expressions of the forward glider personnel were plainly visible. Each glider carried about twenty airmen. Before returning to base, the tow planes climbed to altitude and released the gliders, allowing them to circle downward before coming in for landing.

The bombing range was also utilized as a gunnery strafing range for the P-40 fighter aircraft. Three or four planes at a time would approach from the west at an elevation of perhaps 2,000 feet, continue eastward for a mile or so, bank sharply to the right in steep descent, line up on a westerly heading, level off at about a hundred feet above the ground and fire 50-calibre machine guns at pyramid-shaped fixed targets.

Several accidents, mostly fatal, occurred during these exercises. One B-24 bomber crashed nine miles north of town one afternoon, killing all ten airmen. Workers in nearby broomcorn fields described the bomber as being on a northward heading at an altitude of about two thousand feet when it started a slow leftward roll. The plane dropped sharply as the roll approached 90-deg and flew into the ground. It was assumed to be a mechanical failure of the control cables. Another crashed and burned north of Clovis, and there were others that crashed in the general area. Two twin-engine trainer planes crashed during high wind and low visibility conditions, with the loss of four lives each. One P-40 fighter plane crashed and burned one mile south of our home, killing the pilot. The plane was observed by passengers in a school bus as the pilot unsuccessfully attempted to pull out of a dive. Dog tags identified him as "Billy Williams."

The advent of radar, advances in aviation technology and the huge manufacturing effort provided the aircraft and essentials for our aviators. However, our greatest assets were the airmen themselves.

They came from the big cities, from the towns and small villages; they came from across the countryside. They were heroes—all!

THE MEN AND THEIR AIRCRAFT

The lives of twenty-four aviators became forever intertwined in the skies over Ploesti, Rumania, in 1944 during which a pair of bomber crews, an aerial photographer and a fighter pilot engaged in aerial warfare in the deadliest air battles the world had ever known. The odds of surviving these almost daily encounters were somewhere between slim and none. Yet, by some miracle, most of these brave and courageous airmen lived through the horrific campaigns and returned home as World War II drew to a close. Three were buried on foreign soil near where they sacrificed their lives. Their stories follow in the chronological sequence of their involvement in the war.

THE *SHILAY-LEE* (B-24 BOMBER)

- Lt. Francis "Mike" Boyle, pilot
- Lt. Frederick "Sam" Moore, copilot
- Lt. Robert Barker, navigator
- Lt. Julius Altvater, bombardier
- Sgt. Wayne Simmons, radioman/nose gunner
- Sgt. Vernon MacNeil, ball turret gunner
- Sgt. Hugh Moore, tail gunner
- Sgt. Robert Bluhm, waist gunner
- Sgt. James Benardini, flight engineer/top turret gunner

- Sgt. Allen Christianson, waist gunner
- Cpl. Douglas Millar, aerial photographer

Crew of the *Shilay-Lee; Front row, L to R*: Boyle, Barker, Altvater, Benardini; *Standing, L to R*: F. Moore, Bluhm, Simmons, H. Moore, Christianson, MacNeil

THE *HEARTS AND FLOWERS* (B-17 BOMBER)

- Lt. Leo Bollei, pilot
- F/O Sidney Fisher, copilot
- Lt. William F. Karlovitz, navigator
- Lt. Keith R. Winder, bombardier
- T/Sgt. Wilburn W. Seal, top turret gunner/engineer
- S/Sgt. Raymond Crouch, left waist gunner
- T/Sgt. Edward A. Buffington, radio operator/gunner
- S/Sgt. Joseph J. Cutrone, right waist gunner
- S/Sgt. Jack R. Haney, tail gunner
- S/Sgt. Leslie W. Jensen, ball turret gunner
- Lt. John B. Donner, original pilot
- S/Sgt Robert Jackson, original radio operator

SQUEEZIE (P-51)

- Major Stanley L. DeGeer, pilot

Theirs was a difficult duty, starting when they were roused from their beds at around four AM—almost every morning—in preparation for the day's mission, having to contend with rain, mud and the cold. Well before dawn, each was in his aircraft getting ready for whatever rendezvous that lay ahead. Sixty or more bombers usually flew out on a particular mission, and other missions were sometimes prescribed for the other bomber groups and squadrons on any given day. Bombing missions were carried out against strategic and priority targets including railroad marshalling yards, industrial centers, sea ports, petroleum facilities and other targets on which the Nazi regime relied for their war effort. Friendly fighter pilots flew escort for the bombers, made strafing runs on railroads and trains, factories, supply depots and shipping docks and launched attacks on other targets of opportunity. Enemy fighter pilots took to the sky to fight off American bombers in defense of their factories, oil refineries and other sites required by the Nazis to keep their war machines operating.

Crew of the *Hearts and Flowers; Front row, L to R*: Karlovitz, Winder, Donner, Bollei; *Standing, L to R*: Cutrone, Crouch, Haney, Jackson, Seal, Jensen

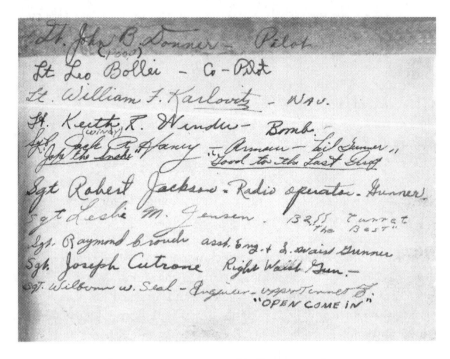

Signatures on reverse side of previous photo

Maj. Stanley L. DeGeer, P-51 pilot

The Nazis had overrun most of Western Europe by 1942, pushing the Allied Forces—England, France and the United States—across the Mediterranean Sea into Africa. Following almost a year of impasse warring in the African deserts, the accelerating production of American bomber and fighter aircraft helped turn the tide, resulting in the retreat of General Erwin Rommel's *Afrika Korps* back across the Mediterranean Sea.

The allied air operations in the MTO operated from bases in North Africa during which time allied infantry and marine divisions were converging to retake Sicily and the lower part of Italy. Fierce fighting took place in Italy and the south of France—between the Germans (to the north) and the Allied Forces (to the south)—until the Germans were driven northward, permitting the 15th Air Force to begin establishing bases in southern Italy in late December, 1943. Flight times for missions were reduced by several hours—an incredible achievement—by flying out of Italy rather than Africa.

The *Shilay-Lee* and *Hearts and Flowers* were two of more than a thousand bombers in the 15th Air Force under the command of Major General Jimmy Doolittle. The '*15th*' was constituted on October 31, 1943, and activated the following day as a heavy bombardment force. It was structured into wings, groups and squadrons. Each bomber squadron (BS) had twenty or more heavy bombers, for a total of about eighty bombers in each of the twenty-one bomber groups (BG). 'Wings' consisted of three or four BGs operating as a single unit. The totals for each squadron varied from week to week, depending on combat losses and the arrival of replacement aircraft and men. The organization of the 15th Air Force by groups and squadrons is included in Appendix "A."

THE B-17 FLYING FORTRESS

The B-17 Flying Fortress was one of the two types of "heavy" bombers employed by the United States during World War II. It was first designed in 1934 by Boeing Aircraft Company. Over the following years, it was further upgraded and modified, especially after the United States entered World War II, evolving into the "G" model that saw most of the action in the war. More than 8,000 B-17G Flying Fortresses were manufactured at the Boeing Aircraft Company in Seattle, Washington. Only thirty B-17s were in existence when Hitler's military forces invaded

Poland in 1939. By the time full production of the B-17 got into full swing over the next two to three years, Boeing, Douglas and Lockheed Vega Aircraft were turning them out in large numbers.

The Flying Fortress was easily recognized by its low-wing configuration and large single rudder with the long dorsal fin. The aircraft utilized the conventional 'tail-dragger' type retractable landing gear, with the main forward wheels suspended from the inboard engine housings. The B-17G sported a chin gun turret that was effective in combating frontal attacks from enemy fighter planes. Unlike the B-24, the B-17 had paired bombay doors that hung out into the airstream when open, producing drag during the pass over the target zone. There were occasions when one or both doors became jammed from flak or gunfire, with the plane having to return home at higher power settings in order to offset the induced drag, thus consuming precious fuel.

The four big engines and large propellers generated so much noise in flight that conversation was quite difficult. However, the B-17 was equipped with an intercom system through which the pilot (flight chief) could communicate with the crew, and the crew with one another. This wired system had plug-in receptacles near each crewman's duty station and at strategic places throughout the aircraft so the crew could remain connected. Their flight caps/helmets were equipped with headsets for listening and throat microphones for speaking. This made it possible for a crewmember to move about the aircraft without losing voice contact with other crewmembers.

Upon reaching elevations of 15,000 feet and higher, temperatures dropped dramatically, requiring crewmembers to wear heavy fur-lined suits for protection against the cold. At ordinary cruise elevations during missions, the temperature was -20° F or lower. Later aircraft were fitted with special receptacles into which electric flight suits could be connected. These and other aircraft of that era didn't have pressurized cabins, so crewmen were required to wear oxygen masks in the rarified atmosphere at the elevations they ordinarily flew. The masks had to be cleared of ice from time to time, due to frozen moisture from breathing. A total of 12,731 B-17s were produced.

Specifications for the B-17 were fairly similar to those of the B-24 Liberator.

B-17 Flying Fortresses bombing German factory

B-17G SPECIFICATIONS

Wingspan	104 ft
Length	74 ft
Weight (empty)	36,000 lbs
Weight (max)	54,000 lbs
Speed (cruise)	170–200 mph
Speed (max)	287 mph
Range	2,000 miles
Ceiling	35,000 ft

Although the Flying Fortress had slightly less performance characteristics than the Liberator, it appears to be the more preferred of the two bombers due to its ruggedness and overall qualities. Numerous

Flying Fortresses returned safely from bombing missions with large sections of wing and tail surfaces missing. This aircraft was much easier to fly, and the chances of surviving a crash landing were better due in part to the Liberator's greater tendency to catch fire. Overall, though, the Liberator was faster, could carry a larger payload and had a longer range.

THE B-24 LIBERATOR

The B-24 Liberator was designed by Consolidated Aircraft Company in San Diego, California, in early 1939. The first prototype took flight later that year but wasn't formally introduced until 1941, at which time there was great demand for heavy bombers by the Allied Forces in Europe. Production accelerated rapidly as England and France pressed for high performance heavy bombers. The United States was the only country in the world that could design, test and produce warplanes over a short time span. Several factories received contracts from the federal government for mass production of warplanes.

B-24 Liberators bombing oil refineries at Ploesti, Rumania

Those factories that produced the B-24 included the Ford Motor Company Plant at Willow Run, Michigan, Consolidated Aircraft

Company at San Diego, California, and at its newer plant near Fort Worth, Texas, North American Aviation at Dallas, Texas, and Douglas Aircraft Company at Tulsa, Oklahoma. Ford Motor Company's Willow Run Plant, the largest factory in the world, produced the greatest number of B-24 Liberators.

This aircraft, distinguished by its large twin rudders and shoulder wing placement, was dubbed the "Flying Boxcar." Early models sported twin 50-calibre gun placements—one pair each in the nose (forward firing), in the tail position, at the left and right waist positions and at the top and belly turret positions, for a total of twelve machine guns. The B-24 was fitted with retractable tricycle landing gear—a nose wheel and two main wheels back of the inboard engine housings. It was also fitted with roller type bombay doors that opened and closed in the same manner as roller type garage doors. The advantage of this type door was that it didn't drag in the airstream when in the open position.

The power plants consisted of four 14-cylinder, double-row radial, air-cooled Pratt & Whitney engines providing 1,000 HP each, or 4,000 total HP. Later models were upgraded to 1,200 HP engines by the addition of exhaust-powered super chargers. Each engine drove a three-blade controllable-pitch propeller—low pitch providing maximum RPM for take-off and climb performance and higher pitch for cruising at altitude. Fuel tanks were located in the upper fuselage near the wing root attachments.

One disadvantage of the B-24 was its handling difficulty, due in part to the larger control surfaces that required greater physical effort by the pilots. It was reported that this aircraft was also more difficult to maintain in tight formation than the B-17.

The fuselage consisted of five sections, or zones—nose, flight deck, bombay, waist, and tail sections. The pilot and copilot were located side-by-side on the flight deck; the top turret gunner position was atop the aircraft just back of the flight deck; the bombardier and nose gunner were located forward in the nose; back of the flight deck was the bombay where the bombs were stowed; a narrow catwalk ran forward to aft along the center; the radioman sat in a small niche next to the bombay, and the navigator operated from a position below and forward of the flight deck; the waist gunners were located near window ports in the midsection of the fuselage; the tail gunner was located in a small cubicle at the rear and the ball turret gunner was located on the underside of the plane at the "belly" position. Unlike the B-17 bomber, the ball turret could be retracted inside the fuselage when not in combat mode.

The B-24 was noisy in flight. The four engines and large propellers generated so much noise that communication was difficult without the use of headsets and throat microphones. The pilot communicated with the crew via the plane's intercom system, and the crew could also communicate with each other. The craft wasn't pressurized, so the crew wore heavy insulated attire when cruising above 14,000 feet. Later versions were equipped with electric flight suits. Cruise elevation during bombing missions was usually between 17,000 and 28,000 feet where the temperature was -20° F or lower. Oxygen masks were required when cruising above 10,000 feet.

A total of 18, 482 B-24s were produced. The performance of the Liberator was similar to, but slightly better than, that of the B-17 Flying Fortress.

B-24H SPECIFICATIONS

Wingspan	110 ft
Length	68 ft
Weight (empty)	36,000 lbs
Weight (loaded)	65,000 lbs
Speed (cruise)	215 mph
Speed (max)	290 mph
Range	2,100–3,700 mi
Ceiling	28,000 ft

The payload for the Liberator was 8,000 pounds of bombs for most missions but could be increased to more than 12,000 pounds for shorter missions. The flight time for missions generally ranged between seven and ten hours each during which the crewmen were zipped into their flight suits with oxygen masks covering their faces—a very long time without a meal or access to a bathroom. Crewmen reported having to periodically clear their oxygen masks of heavy frost that accumulated due to frozen moisture from breathing. Removal of the oxygen mask for more than a minute or two would result in unconsciousness followed by death.

AMERICAN FIGHTER AIRCRAFT OF WORLD WAR II

The P-51 Mustang fighter plane was considered the supreme fighter aircraft of World War II. It was the fastest, most maneuverable and effective propeller-driven fighter aircraft of all time. It was preceded by a number of other fighter aircraft including the Curtiss P-40 Warhawk, Republic P-47 Thunderbolt, Bell P-39 Airacobra, Grumman F4F Wildcat, Vought-Sikorsky F4U Corsair, and the twin-engine Lockheed P-38 Lightning.

MAJOR AMERICAN PURSUIT AIRCRAFT

Curtiss P-40	Warhawk	1938	Land based
Bell P-39	Airacobra	1939	Land based
Grumman F4F	Wildcat/Hellcat	1940	Carrier based
Vought-Sikorsky F4U	Corsair	1940	Land and Carrier based
Republic P-47	Thunderbolt	1941	Land based
Lockheed P-38	Lightning	1941	Land based
North American P-51	Mustang	1942	Land based

At the time of the assault on Pearl Harbor in late 1941, the Bell P-39 and Curtiss P-40 were the principle fighter planes in the American arsenal. Other fighter aircraft were in various stages of development and testing. America was years behind the German and Japanese aircraft programs, with American fighter aircraft barely able to hold their own against the superior enemy aircraft already in service. This changed abruptly.

Production of all types of aircraft accelerated rapidly—almost overnight—as Ford, General Motors, Chrysler, Packard, and other motor companies switched over to manufacturing war machines as new assembly plants sprouted up all around the country. American fighter aircraft were upgraded and modified frequently in order to achieve the highest levels of performance under combat conditions. The fighters that performed the best were produced in higher quantities while production of the others dropped off.

Before long, American fighter aircraft were able to match the best enemy fighter planes in the skies. The F4U Corsair became a dreaded death machine to the Japanese in the Pacific. The P-38 Lightning and P-47 Thunderbolt wreaked havoc against enemy fighter planes in both the Pacific and European theaters. As the war drug on, there was a need for escort fighter planes to accompany bombers carrying out missions against targets deep inside Germany and Europe, and also in the Pacific. American fighter aircraft had limited ranges and could remain in the skies for only two to three hours—far insufficient to accompany the bombers all the way to their targets. A new fighter aircraft was desperately needed.

BIRTH OF THE P-51 MUSTANG

The water-cooled Allison 12-cylinder engine concept evolved from the 1920s as a 'hot rod' power plant for racing cars but was soon shelved due to the Great Depression. It was revived in 1938 when such an engine was needed for three earlier fighter aircraft being developed—the twin-engine Lockheed P-38, the Bell mid-engine mounted P-39, and the Curtiss P-40. The radiator on the P-51 was mounted on the belly, just below and extending back of the wing attachment. The following account was related to the author by Dr. John H. Altseimer, aeronautical engineer and long time personal associate who was a member of the engineer team that designed and engineered the original P-51 Mustang.

In April of 1940, a small group of America's top aeronautical engineers assembled in a closed room within a secure hangar in the California desert with military guards standing by. The project brought together the top design engineers from several companies working together under the umbrella of North American Aviation. They were given an assignment—to design, construct and test-fly a new fighter aircraft far superior to any such aircraft in existence—in 120 days! This was a formidable task, but these engineers weren't intimidated. They set about their work diligently.

American top military brass met with this elite group to discuss parameters and specifications for configuring the new fighter plane. The British had placed orders for this yet-to-be-built aircraft, with specific requirements regarding speed, maneuverability, climb performance, range, service ceiling, payload, durability and pilot safety. Sketches, mathematical figures and theoretical projections were developed on a blackboard that covered most of the front wall of the workroom. At the end of each long day, attachment screws were removed, the blackboard was flipped around facing the wall, and the screws were replaced. Military personnel escorted the engineers to their bus, and they were transported back to civilization. Military police remained in the hangar to keep watch over the premises while others guarded the exterior. There would be no one—absolutely no one—permitted to approach the hangar.

Each morning, the engineers arrived for another workday. Lunch was brought in so there would be neither time wasted nor casual exposure to outsiders. The project was totally secret and would remain that way. The blackboard ritual was repeated daily, with the plans secreted next to the wall each night. None of the team was permitted to make any notes or draw any plans; the only plans were those developed on the blackboard.

Over the space of several weeks, working plans for the new aircraft were completed at which time one set of construction drawings and specifications was produced on paper. They were stored in a secure vault when not being used by the team. Newly designed components were ordered to be manufactured immediately—first priority—with no time of delay. Three regular production Allison V-1710 series (V-12 configuration) liquid-cooled engines having specific modifications were ordered from General Motors. A large, three-bladed propeller was called for, so special reduction gearboxes had to be constructed for the engine-to-propeller configuration. Other airframe and related components were ordered, as were off-the-shelf avionics (instrumentation) and other apparatus. Propellers are discussed in Appendix G.

The P-51 had many unique features, not the least of which was the 'laminar flow' airfoil design of the wings and the belly location for the radiator. A word about airfoils is included in Appendix F.

On the 117th day following the start of the project, three prototype "XP-51" aircraft sat side by side near the hangar—3 days ahead of schedule! Before the first test flight got off the ground, the reduction gearbox failed and the flight had to be aborted. The second and third test planes took to the air without problem and fulfilled the terms of the project—one of the most dramatic events in aviation history! Production got underway at North American Aviation, and the first units were delivered to the Royal Air Force in early 1941.

The North American P-51 Mustang was an instant success. It was incredibly fast, had a long range and outperformed other fighter aircraft. It was the first escort fighter that could accompany a flight of bombers from England to targets in Europe and return. Herman Goering, Adolph Hitler's aviation chief, upon observing P-51s flying over Berlin, was credited with saying, *"This is the beginning of the end."* For the first time, enemy fighters didn't have free range to attack Allied bombers, and the P-51 proved to be more than a match for the best German aircraft. The P-51 was designed so efficiently that it was more than 30 mph faster than the British Supermarine Spitfire that had the more powerful Rolls-Royce Merlin engine.

The P-51 was modified from time to time, evolving into the P-51D that continued past the end of the war. A major modification was the new powerplant—the British Rolls Royce Merlin engine, driving a large four-blade propeller having a 10-ft. 9-in. diameter—giving the "D" model an increased top speed, a ceiling of over 40,000 feet and greatly improved performance in other areas. Packard Motor Company built the Rolls Royce V-1650-7 engines under license from the British Rolls Royce Company. One innovation of the P-51D was its bubble canopy, giving pilots a 360-degree field of view.

The P-51s were ferried to Europe in groups by mostly women pilots flying the northern ferry route through Greenland to the U.K. The author was acquainted with one of those pilots, Ruth Deck, whose parents lived in Melrose. Her father, Rev. George Deck, was pastor of the local Nazarene Church during the war. Ruth rarely had opportunity to return home during these years but, on one such occasion, she brought the author a calendar-size photo of a P-51A she'd ferried to England.

P-51 SPECIFICATIONS

Wingspan	37 ft.
Length	32 ft. 3 in.
Weight (empty)	7,635 lbs.
Weight (max)	12.100 lbs.
Powerplant. 1.490 HP	V-12, Packard Merlin V-1650-7
Airspeed (cruise)	363 mph
Airspeed (max)	437 mph
Range	1,650 miles (with external tanks)
Ceiling	41,900 ft.

P-51D Mustang; DeGeer's "Squeezie"

MESSERSCHMITT ME-109 (AKA, BF-109)

The Me-109 was probably the best and most feared German fighter aircraft of World War II. Designed in 1934, by Willy Messerschmitt, it was originally powered by the Rolls Royce Kestrel engine. In 1935, the Me-109 won the world fighter class competition. As the war heated up across Europe, the aircraft was refitted with the 1,150 HP Daimler-Benz 12-cylinder liquid-cooled powerplant.

The "*109*" first saw action during the Spanish Civil War of 1936–39. After the British Spitfire fighter aircraft specifications became known to the Germans, the Me-109 went through numerous modifications aimed at improving its performance, including later engine versions and better handling characteristics. After engaging the Spitfire and Hawker Hurricane fighters in actual combat, it was found that the Spitfire was faster and more maneuverable at elevations up to 15,000 feet but, that at higher elevations, the *109* outperformed the Spitfire. It was also found that the slower Hurricane was more rugged and difficult to shoot down in combat. On the other hand, the *109* was not as rugged and was easily shot down whenever a few shots found their mark.

Although fast and highly maneuverable, the *109* was a fuel guzzler. In operation, it could remain in the air for only about 90 minutes before having to land and refuel. Late in the war, some *109s* were fitted with exterior tanks in order to increase their time in flight, but the drag induced by the tanks resulted in poorer performance and were for the most part counterproductive.

More Me-109s were produced during the war than any other aircraft. It was recognized as the backbone of the *Luftwaffe* throughout the conflict.

ME-109G SPECIFICATIONS

Wingspan	32 ft. 6 in.
Length	29 ft. 7 in.
Weight (empty)	5,893
Weight (loaded)	7,495
Powerplant	1,450 HP V-12 Daimler-Benz DB- 605A-1
Airspeed (cruise)	365 mph
Airspeed (max)	398 mph
Range	528 mi. (1,000 mi. w/drop tank)
Ceiling	39,370 ft.

Messerschmitt Me-109

CREW OF THE "*SHILAY-LEE*"

Ten courageous young men—part of a much larger group—arrived at Gowen Field just south of Boise, Idaho, during the summer of 1943 to train as members of a tightly-knit family of warriors working together as a fighting team—the crew of the *Shilay-Lee*, a B-24 heavy bomber. They came from the big cities, small towns and communities. They came from across the sprawling landscape of the greatest nation on the planet, having already completed basic and advanced training in special skills as gunners, pilots, radiomen, navigators, bombardiers and engineers. These were America's finest.

They endured hazardous and grueling training for more than a year and were finally ready and anxious to leap into the abysmal European firestorm generated by madman Adolph Hitler and the Nazis. These were the men who placed themselves in harm's way in order that Freedom would be preserved at any cost.

FREEDOM IS NOT FREE, it comes at a price; America is greatly indebted to those brave soldiers of every era, of every branch, whether in war or in peace, who sacrificed much, even their lives, that we might live in a free society. Except for those who answered the call to defend our liberty, who stood between us and certain destruction, we would be an enslaved people speaking some strange tongue.

THE TEAM

- Lt. Francis Boyle, pilot
- Lt. Frederick Moore, copilot
- Lt. Robert Barker, navigator
- Lt. Julius Altvater, bombardier
- Sgt. Robert Bluhm, right waist gunner
- Sgt. Hugh Moore, tail turret gunner
- Sgt. James Benardini, flight engineer/top turret gunner
- Sgt. Allen Christianson, left waist gunner
- Sgt. Vernon MacNeil, ball turret gunner
- Sgt. Wayne Simmons, radioman/nose turret gunner

Two living survivors from the ten-member crew were located in late 2007—James N. Benardini (living in Florida) and Vernon MacNeil (living in Idaho)—after which Vernon shared his stories and feelings about his involvement in World War II.

Francis "Mike" Boyle, born on July 17, 1918, in Grand Haven, Michigan, was an outstanding student and football player who graduated from high school in 1937 at the height of the Great Depression. Over the next four years, he worked as a welder and flame cutter, possibly at an automotive factory. At the age of twenty-three, after completing one year of college and working as a lifeguard, he enlisted in the army at Kalamazoo, Michigan, on September 17, 1941. His enlistment records indicate that he was single and was inducted as a private on track to becoming an officer.

Mike reported to the Army Training Center at Ft. Warren, Wyoming, for basic training. He scored well and was accepted into the Aviation Cadet training program at Santa Ana, California. Less than eight months after enlisting, he receiving his *Pilots Wings* on May 5, 1942, was commissioned 2nd Lieutenant and assigned to the Army Air Base at La Junta, Colorado.

Being a proficient pilot—and a few years older than most others in his group—Mike may have been assigned to train new pilots entering the Aviation Cadet program over the next fifteen months. In any case, he arrived at Gowen Army Air Base in Idaho in early August of the following year.

Frederick "Sam" Moore was born at Richmond, Virginia, in 1919. After graduation from high school in 1937, he married Iris and worked as a machinist. On December 19, 1941, Sam was required to register for the draft. He was allowed a deferment until September of 1943, probably due to working in a strategic job (i.e., aircraft manufacturing). However, he signed up in the Army Air Corps Reserves and was inducted on May 12, 1942, four months prior to the end of his draft extension.

Sam was a tall handsome guy, never one to mince words. He applied himself diligently and passed both the physical and academic exams with flying colors. Sam was among those selected to advance to Aviation Cadet School. This was pure excitement, for he would train to become a pilot. In September of 1942, Sam's class started training in a number of different aircraft including simple, single-engine Fairchild PT-19 and Stearman BT-13 trainers. Those who didn't wash out advanced to the higher performing AT-6 trainer and the twin-engine A-26 light bomber before finally moving on to the heavy bomber.

Upon graduation from flight school, most of the group was sent on to intensive training at various Army Air Corps bases stocked with four-engine B-24 or B-17 heavy bombers. Sam probably remained as a flight instructor for the younger cadets up through mid-summer of 1943, at which time he was transferred to Gowen Army Air Base at Boise, Idaho.

Robert J. "Bob" Barker enlisted in the military on January 10, 1941—almost a year prior to the Japanese attack on Pearl Harbor. He was born in New Jersey on June 4, 1919, and was living in West Orange at the time of his enlistment. Bob graduated from high school in 1937, completed one year of college and was single and working as a welder and flame cutter at the time of his enlistment in the Army Air Corps. At some point after completing basic training in the spring of 1941, he tried out for the Aviation Cadet program. Following intensive training and classroom studies, his education, skills and experience resulted in his being sent to school for advanced training as a navigator.

Navigation school was not for the slow or timid. It involved long, rigorous hours in the classroom—poring over maps and working out mathematical problems. The fate of the bomber crew lay in the ability of the navigator to determine an accurate course to a target or other destination and to direct the plane safely back to its home base. Bob graduated and was assigned to Gowen Army Air Base in Idaho in mid-summer of 1943.

Julius A. "Al" Altvater had the most colorful and diverse experience from among the crew. He was born in New York City on July 26, 1920, and grew up working in his father's domestic business, mixing and packaging various compounds for automotive applications. Al completed only two years of high school but otherwise self-educated himself through hard work and dealing with clientele in and around the big city during the years of the Great Depression—when survival was a day to day affair. He moved on to mechanical and manufacturing jobs, had to deal with more than his share of adversity, got into more than his share of difficulties and, on July 21, 1941—five days before his 19th birthday—enlisted in the Army Air Corps in New York City.

Al didn't qualify for the Aviation Cadet program for pilot training—no college degree, no high school diploma—so, greatly disappointed, he signed up for assignment to the Philippines. Then, out of the blue, opportunity knocked at his door, and he jumped at the chance for transfer to the Panama Canal Zone in August. This action undoubtedly saved him from being on the Bataan Death March.

Basic training got underway shortly but, on December 7, the Japanese attacked Pearl Harbor. Not long afterward, the requirements for entering Air Cadet School were lowered so that anyone passing the tests could qualify for the program. This time, Al passed the test easily and was back in Texas at the Aviation Cadet Center in February of 1942. He washed out as a pilot so was sent to the Army Air Corps Bombardier School at San Angelo, Texas. In early August of 1943, he was assigned to Gowen Army Air Base in Idaho.

Robert M. "Bob" Bluhm was born at Herkimer, Kansas on June 30, 1920, and was living near Quincy, Illinois, at the time of his enlistment in the Army Air Corps at Peoria on September 11, 1942. He had completed high school and was working on a farm, was single and had no dependents.

Bob passed through basic training and was assigned to Nevada or Arizona for gunnery training—he had no desire to become a pilot. Nine months later, he arrived at Gowen Army Air Base in Idaho to take on the assignment as a gunner on heavy bombers.

Hugh M. Moore was born at Philadelphia, Pennsylvania, on June 27, 1917. He graduated from high school in 1935 and worked as an accountant up until the time he enlisted in the Army Air Corps on January 3, 1942. At twenty-six years of age, he was older than most of the others. Following basic training, he may have been assigned to train younger enlistees on their way to the war zone.

By early August of the following year, Hugh was assigned to Gowen Army Air Base in Idaho to take on the role of gunner on heavy bombers.

James N. "Moose" Benardini was living in Ohio at the time of his enlistment in the Army Air Corps during the fall of 1942. He was twenty years of age. His enlistment files are missing from the NARA National Archives Database, although some later records, including his serial number and rank, are found.

After completing basic training, Moose completed Aircraft Maintenance School and received his Flight Engineer certification several months later. He was in aircraft gunnery training in either Nevada or Arizona, up until August of 1943, when he was transferred to Gowen Army Air Base for gunnery training on heavy bombers. As of this date— July 1, 2010—he appears to be one of only two surviving members of the ten-man crew featured in this chapter. Attempts to communicate with him or his wife, Dorothy, were unsuccessful, and the author doesn't wish to intrude into their lives.

Allen G. "Chris" Christianson was living at Fertile, Minnesota, when he enlisted in the Army Air Corps in 1942. His enlistment files are missing from the NARA National Archives Database, although later records include his serial number and rank.

Chris would have gone to basic training for several months, followed by gunnery training, after which he arrived at Gowen Army Air Base in Idaho in early August of 1943, assuming the role of gunner on heavy bombers. He appears to be living in Oregon.

Vernon R. "Mac" MacNeil was born in the farming community of Rockland, Idaho, in 1923. At the age of nineteen, having completed a year of college, he was on the verge of being drafted, so he elected to enlist in the military. He travelled to Salt Lake City, Utah—a couple of hours by car—enlisted and was inducted into the Army Air Corps on November 28, 1942. Since he was listed as a farmer, he would have received an automatic draft deferment for one year, so that may be why he waited until after the fall harvest of 1942, before enlisting.

Following basic training, Mac was transferred to gunnery school and later assigned to Gowen Army Air Field at Boise, Idaho, in August of 1943. It was here that he was introduced to a four-engine B-24 "Liberator" heavy bomber and nine other crewmen.

Ova Wayne (Seal) Simmons was born on March 7, 1924, in the small farming community of Delhi in southwestern Oklahoma. His mother passed away when he was four years of age, so he grew up living with his maternal grandparents, Luther and Elsie Simmons. He was in his junior year of high school when the Japanese attacked Pearl Harbor, forcing the United States into World War II. Realizing he would be drafted into the military before long, he may have tried to enlist at that time. He did, however, travel to Oklahoma City in early 1942, enlisted in the Army Air Corps and was called to active duty on November 11. His surname was changed from "Seal" to "Simmons" before entering the Air Corps.

After completing boot camp, Wayne was selected for radio school and assigned to a facility for training in radio and electronics. Upon completion, he was sent to a gunnery training facility, probably in Nevada or Arizona, after which he was assigned to Gowen Army Air Field near Boise, Idaho, in early August of 1943.

> [Note: Considerably more is known about Robert Bluhm, Wayne Simmons and Vernon MacNeil due to the author's direct contact with Bluhm's and Simmons's family members and through direct contact with Vernon MacNeil. The author was a high school classmate and friend of Wayne's sister, Nelda Seal, during the years of 1941–46. Nelda provided background information about Wayne through her interaction with him up to the time he entered the Army Air Corps in 1942, and also provided a number of photos. Wayne passed away of brain tumor in 1956, leaving a wife and three young children. The author was fortunate in locating his wife—who remarried several years after Wayne's passing—and their eldest son, Robert Wayne Simmons. The author was equally fortunate in having located

Bluhm's son, Gene Bluhm, who provided numerous photos, documents and other material valuable to this work. Many of the photos and documents in this book are courtesy of Gene Bluhm and Robert Simmons.]

[Gowen Field—originally known as "Boise Air Terminal"—was first planned during the late 1930s. The Army Air Corps selected the site because of its strategic location and the wind conditions for landings and take-offs. Construction began in early 1941, just south of Boise, Idaho, for what was to become a training base for fifty-four medium twin-engine bombers and 3,000 personnel. Nine hundred workers were employed at this base during a critical time when the Great Depression had deeply impacted Boise. The name "Boise" would have brought notoriety to the area, but the government had other ideas. They changed the name to "Gowen Field" in honor of 1st Lt. Paul R. Gowen, a former resident of Caldwell, Idaho, who died when his B-10 twin-engine plane crashed near Panama on July 11, 1938.]

The start of World War II brought on the need for long range bombers in place of the smaller twin-engine bombers. B-17 Flying Fortresses soon became a familiar sight as they flew over Boise while on training missions, dropping 100-lb practice bombs on targets in the surrounding area. In May, 1943, Gowen Field became a training field for B-24 Liberators. Many crews were trained and sent to both the Pacific and European Theaters of War. One of those trainees was movie star James Stewart who had volunteered. He arrived on February 11, 1943, and trained as a pilot. Stewart flew twenty-five bombing missions over Europe in a B-24, rising to the rank of colonel.

Training got underway with the planes flying singly and in groups at both low and high elevations. Gunnery training missions were also carried out, with gunners shooting at sleeve targets towed by twin-engine A-26 light bombers. Bombing training was carried out over ground targets located on special bombing ranges across the Idaho countryside.

The crew became 'family', with the airmen learning to work together as a team, after which they were sent to Fairmont Army Air Field near Geneva, Nebraska, where they were assigned to the 727th Squadron of the 451st Bombardment Group. They met members of the other squadrons and further trained in their assigned roles. In late November, they were summoned to the flight lines and assigned their own plane—a brand new, olive-drab painted B-24H. This would be their plane for the duration.

Their new plane was the latest version to roll off the assembly line at the new Consolidated Aircraft Company plant near Fort Worth, Texas. A major innovation was the bubble nose turret that sported two 50-caliber machine guns. Their aircraft—#41-29239—was dubbed the "*Shilay-Lee*", after an archaic Irish wooden weapon, or club (the *shillelagh*).

The new nose turret caught Wayne Simmons's attention, so he inquired of Lt. Mike Boyle whether he might be assigned the nose turret position. It had a rather confined space, and Wayne's stature seemed to fit well, so Lt. Boyle gave him the assignment. As radio operator, Wayne was free to move back and forth between the radio compartment and the nose turret.

Vernon MacNeil was slender and nimble. During flight, he was often rolled up like a doughnut in the cramped quarters of the ball turret on the underside of the plane. Unlike the B-17 Flying Fortress, however, the ball turret was drawn up into the fuselage during flight and was only lowered to the belly position whenever the plane was flying in combat role.

The training flights out of Fairmont Army Airfield provided the crew with the genuine wintry type flight conditions they would encounter in Italy several weeks later.

CREW OF THE *"HEARTS AND FLOWERS"*

Ten of our finest—young men from across the Heartland of America—joined together at Dyersburg Army Air Corps Base in Tennessee the first week of November in 1943, after having undergone intensive training in their particular specialties at other bases around the country. They had passed through rigorous basic training followed by advanced training as pilots, navigators, bombardiers, radio operators, flight engineers and gunners. Over the next thirty days, they worked together diligently, from daylight until after dark, sharpening their skills aboard the B-17F Flying Fortress heavy bomber, transitioning into a family, a team of experts, ready to take on the German Luftwaffe and other Nazi forces in Europe.

> *"The Tree of Liberty must be refreshed from time to time with the blood of patriots and tyrants."*
>
> *Thomas Jefferson*

THE TEAM

- Lt. John B. Donner, pilot
- Lt. Leo Bollei, copilot
- Lt. William F. Karlovitz, navigator
- Lt. Keith R. Winder, bombardier

- Sgt. Wilburn W. Seal, flight engineer/top turret gunner
- Sgt. Raymond Crouch, left waist gunner
- Sgt. Joseph J. Cutrone, right waist gunner
- Sgt. Robert L. Jackson, radioman/gunner
- Sgt. Jack R. Haney, tail gunner
- Sgt. Leslie M. Jenson, ball turret gunner

[The crew make-up changed after the seventh combat mission. Lt. Donner and Sgt. Jackson were transferred to other aircraft, and two late comers were brought in to fill the vacancies. Lt. Bollei was moved from the copilot to pilot position, and Flight Officer Sidney Fisher was assigned the copilot position. Sgt Edward Buffington filled the radioman and gunner position vacated by Sgt. Jackson.]

Two of the original crewmembers were located in 2007—Leo Bollei (living in Michigan) and Jack R. Haney (living in Washington). Who were these brave men who stepped forward to defend American lives and liberty during our nation's great time of need?

John B. "Jack" Donner was born in Pennsylvania in 1918, shortly after the end of World War I. He was living in Michigan at the outbreak of World War II and appears to have worked for the railroad as a telegraph and telephone installer. He had completed one year of college at the time of his enlistment in the Army Air Corps on April 12, 1942. Jack passed the physical and academic exams, making him eligible for the Aviation Cadet program. He was called up in early November and reported to the cadet training base in Indiana where he met and trained with Leo Bollei. They learned to fly in the Stearman BT-13, advancing to the more powerful North American AT-6 trainer and finally learning to fly the B-17 Flying Fortress.

Leo Bollei was born in Michigan in 1921, and was 21 years of age at the time of his enlistment into the Army Air Corps on May 13, 1942. He was called to active duty in early November. He had completed four years of high school, was single and working as a machinist, possibly in the automotive industry. He passed the physical and academic exams handily and was accepted into the Aviation Cadet training program. It was at the cadet training center in Indiana where Leo met up with John Donner and learned to fly the Stearman PT-13, the North American AT-6 trainer and the B-17 Flying Fortress. Both Bollei and Donner received their 'wings' and were promoted to 2nd Lieutenant. They drove back home together and, after a brief leave, were sent to Salt Lake City, Utah, in late July of 1943, where they met up with two new team mates—Keith Winder and William Karlovitz.

Keith Winder, the eldest of the crew, was born in Ohio in 1916. He was twenty-six years of age at the time of his enlistment at Cleveland, Ohio, on April 24, 1942. He had completed two years of college, was single and may have been working in the motion picture industry at the time. Keith completed basic training, followed by training as a bombardier, and was promoted to 2nd Lieutenant. He was sent to Salt Lake City, Utah, where he met up with Donner, Bollei and Karlovitz.

William F. "Bill" Karlovitz was born in Illinois in 1917. He had completed four years of high school at the time of his enlistment at Chicago, Illinois, on November 26, 1941—less than two weeks prior to the Japanese attack on Pearl Harbor. Bill was single and may have worked as a shipping clerk and laboratory technician. Following basic training, he was sent for advanced navigation training, graduated and was promoted to 2nd Lieutenant. He undoubtedly possessed high mathematical skills for this assignment. He, too, arrived at Salt Lake City, Utah, to join Donner, Bollei and Winder as the officer team for a B-17 Flying Fortress heavy bomber.

Raymond Crouch was born in Missouri in 1917. He was twenty-five years of age and living in Illinois when he enlisted at La Fayette, Indiana, on February 23, 1942. He had completed four years of high school, was married but had no dependants. Raymond completed basic training and was sent to gunnery school, possibly in Nevada. Upon graduation in October, he was assigned to Dyersburg, Tennessee, for aircraft crew training.

Joseph J. Cutrone was born and lived in New York when he enlisted in the Army Air Corps in 1942. After graduation from basic training, he was sent to gunnery school and later transferred to Dyersburg, Tennessee, in October for aircraft crew training.

Robert L. Jackson, a native of Texas, enlisted in the Army Air Corps in 1942. He completed basic training, followed by training to become a radio operator. He was sent to Dyersburg, Tennessee, in October for aircraft crew training aboard a B-17 Flying Fortress.

Jack R. Haney was born in Montana in 1920. He was living in Yakima, Washington, when he enlisted in the Army Air Corps at Santa

Ana, California on March 15, 1943. Jack had completed three years of college and was a student at the time of his enlistment. He applied for Aviation Cadet School but was selected for aircraft gunnery school following basic training. Jack arrived at Dyersburg Army Air Base in Tennessee in late October for aircraft crew training in a B-17 Flying Fortress.

Leslie Jensen was born in North Dakota in 1919 and was living in Los Angeles, California, when he enlisted in the Army Air Corps on November 30, 1942. He had completed grammar school, was single and working as a surveyor. Following basic training, he was sent for gunnery training and upon completion was transferred to Dyersburg, Tennessee, for training as a gunner in a B-17 Flying Fortress.

Wilburn W. Seal was born at Coleman, Texas, on December 21, 1923. He graduated from high school in May, 1942—five months following the Pearl Harbor assault. He enlisted in the Army Air Corps and was called to active duty on November 2, 1942. Following basic training, he was assigned to the Aircraft Maintenance School at Amarillo, Texas, where he trained as a flight engineer. He was sent to Boeing Aircraft's Flight Engineering and Maintenance School at Seattle, Washington, received his Flight Engineer certification and was promoted to Corporal. Wilburn completed aerial gunnery school at Las Vegas, Nevada, flight training exercises at Salt Lake City, Utah, and was then sent to Dyersburg Army Air Base in Tennessee to begin crew training. It was here that he met up with the rest of the crew.

Sidney Fisher was born in Massachusetts on February 19, 1926. He enlisted in the Army on May 24, 1943, at Springfield. Sidney was seventeen years of age and hadn't yet graduated from high school. Following basic training, he was assigned to the Philippine Scouts division but was soon transferred to the Army Air Force where he qualified for Aviation Cadet School. After receiving his wings, he was immediately sent to the combat zone and assigned as copilot of the *Hearts and Flowers*, replacing Lt. John Donner who had been assigned to take over as pilot on another bomber.

Edward A. Buffington was born in Texas on July 20, 1918, and enlisted in the Army Air Force on October 8, 1942, at the AAF Base in Hondo, Texas. He had completed two years of college and, at twenty-two years of age, was older than most of the other crew. He completed radio and gunnery schools and was sent to the combat zone where he was assigned as radioman and gunner on the *Hearts and Flowers*, replacing Sgt. Robert Jackson who had been transferred to a vacant position on another B-17.

The four officers—Bollei, Donner, Winder and Karlovitz—were transferred to Dyersburg AAF Base, Tennessee, in early November after having completed three weeks of preliminary training in Salt Lake City, Utah. They met up with the eight enlisted men at Dyersburg and begin advanced flight training in the B-17F.

Their next stop was at MacDill AAF Base in Florida where they transitioned to formation flying over the next month, compiling about 200 hours flight time in the B-17 Flying Fortress. They were then sent to Wright Field, Ohio, where the entire 463rd Bombardment Group was assembled. On January 21, 1944, they picked up their own B-17G—#42-31791—for final training prior to deployment to Africa.

Over the next thirty days, the crew of the *Hearts and Flowers* completed final training details and, on February 22, 1944, were deployed to Africa to participate in the MTO.

> [Much more is known about Wilburn W. Seal and Leo Bollei due to the author's involvement with Seal family members and direct contact with Bollei in 2007. The author was a classmate of Wilburn's cousin, Nelda Seal, during 1941 through 1946 and also met with his daughter, Jeanette Seal Keithley, who provided substantial materials—photos, documents, etc… Seal's son, Fred Seal, provided important documentation, including copies of his father's flight training and mission logs, and personal accounts. Woody Crouch, Raymond Crouch's son, provided extensive documentation, photos, and other relative information concerning his father. Woody's graphic and descriptive narrative regarding his father's harrowing war experiences is included in Chapter 10.]

DUTIES OF THE CREWMEN

Each of the ten crewmen on the B-17 and B-24 bombers underwent intensive training in his assigned role but also developed skills and understanding of the functions of the other crewmen. Whenever an unexpected necessity might arise, each man was prepared to take over the role of another. The bombardier might be called on to perform as copilot in the event of the copilot's incapacitation. The top turret gunner might be called on to take over the pilot's position if required. As part of the team, each member was ready and capable to assume another duty resulting from any unanticipated or emergency situation.

THE PILOT AND COPILOT

Lieutenants Leo Bollei, John Donner, Sidney Fisher and Francis Boyle received their pilot certification only after having passed rigorous physical and academic tests followed by intensive flight training in several types of aircraft. Two years of college were required for pilots early in the war, but that restriction was dropped as more and more pilots were required to fly the greatly increasing numbers of aircraft heading into combat.

Each had logged more than two hundred hours flight time in his respective aircraft and had become a highly proficient pilot before going into combat—Bollei, Fisher and Donner in a B-17 and Boyle in a B-24. They knew what action to take whenever an emergency arose, such as an engine failure, malfunction of landing gear, loss of hydraulic system or other aircraft component. They understood navigation, gunnery, bombing and other skills required by individual crewmen. They knew their teams well and realized their individual strengths and weaknesses.

The major responsibility of the pilot was that of flight chief—commander of the aircraft. He was in charge of the ship and made all decisions involving ship and crew. He was a leader and, as such, the crew looked to him for leadership and any instructions handed down.

The B-17 was described by experienced pilots as being simple to fly. The B-24, on the other hand, was noted for being heavy on the controls; that is, lots of muscle was continuously required to keep the aircraft straight and level in flight. This was especially true when the planes were flying in tight formation. Elevator control of the B-24—moving the tail up or down—was described as being very sensitive to slight movements of the control wheel (forward or backward), but rudder control—using the pedals—required a lot of force. After long hours at the controls, the pilots often returned to base tired, worn out.

The two types of bombers didn't always perform well when flying together in formation. Part of the problem was the optimal airspeed of the B-24 being around twenty mph faster than the B-17. As the airspeed of the B-24 was reduced to match that of the B-17, the B-24 became slightly less stable, its movements becoming a bit sloppy. When both types of aircraft were assigned to the same mission, the B-24s were usually grouped at the rear, thus placing them at greater risk for rear attacks from enemy fighter planes.

The bombay doors of the B-17 opened downward into the slipstream when approaching the target and produced considerable drag. The pilot was aware of this and compensated for the added drag by applying more power to the engines while pulling back the control wheel slightly in order to keep the aircraft in straight and level flight. It was imperative to maintain elevation during the approach to the target. The B-24, on the other hand, had garage-type doors that rolled up along the side of the fuselage, rather than extending out into the slipstream, resulting in minimal drag.

Whenever the bombay doors on the B-17 became damaged or otherwise inoperable and stuck in the open position, the pilot had to increase the power settings, consuming precious fuel, in order to keep up with the other planes. If an engine happened to fail, the aircraft was in immediate peril from enemy fighter planes that lurked like ravenous vultures waiting for any plane falling behind the pack. Such plane became an immediate target.

The copilot requirements were the same as the pilot except that he performed as assistant pilot. The main difference was that the copilot generally had less time and experience at piloting; at some point in time, most copilots assumed the roles of pilots after acquiring sufficient experience in combat. In the case of Bollei and Donner, they entered Air Cadet School together, completed pilot training and graduated together. When they arrived to pick up their B-17 bomber, a flip of the coin determined that Donner would be the pilot and Bollei the copilot. Later, when Donner was transferred to fill a pilot vacancy on another B-17, Bollei was moved to the pilot position.

In case of the incapacitation of the pilot, the copilot took on the role of commander.

THE NAVIGATOR

Basic requirements for navigators were the same as for pilots. Two years of college were required early in the war, along with rigorous physical and academic exams. Navigators were generally those who first applied to become pilots; some washed out, but others were selected for their proficiencies and mathematical skills.

Getting to the target and returning to home base rested on the shoulders of Lt. Robert Barker and Lt. William Karlovitz. Their job was probably the most important of all, for each had to know the position of his aircraft with reasonable certainty at all times. In fair weather, their job wasn't as difficult. But, when 'socked in' by clouds, fog or haze—when the ground and landmarks were not visible—the lives of the crew lay in the hands of Karlovitz and Barker. At night, they sighted stars through a sextant to determine their location. During the day, they depended on the sun and instruments, including a magnetic compass, clock, altimeter, and predicted winds aloft. Many aircraft were lost because of poor visibility and insufficient wind data. Among these craft was the *"Lady Be Good,"* a B-24 bomber that encountered unpredicted tailwinds, overshot the Mediterranean Sea and crash-landed 400 miles deep into the Sahara Desert.

Karlovitz and Barker could be called on at any time to take over the position of pilot or copilot. Barker actually took over the copilot position during an emergency situation.

THE BOMBARDIER

Lieutenants Julius Altvater and Keith Winder passed the same rigorous exams as pilots Bollei, Donner, Fisher and Boyle. Altvater was disappointed over washing out as a pilot, but he became a highly competent bombardier on the *Shilay-Lee.* Under extreme duress, with his plane badly shot up and crippled, he stayed at his duty station until dropping the bombs on target—mission accomplished—before going aft to take up the battle to save the ship. By the same token, Winder stayed with his assignment until he'd unloosed the bombs on target before turning to find his aircraft had been badly damaged.

The bombardier was called upon during numerous occasions to take over the pilot or copilot position when one or the other became incapacitated.

THE FLIGHT ENGINEER

The engineer usually occupied the top turret gunner position, for this was the closest duty station to the flight deck—the main cabin of the aircraft where the pilot, copilot and flight instrumentation were located. Sergeants Wilburn Seal and James Benardini sat or stood behind the pilot and copilot during take-off, landing and at other times when requested by the pilot. Seal and Benardini had undergone extensive training in all aspects of their respective aircraft, including several months working at the factories where they were built. They'd passed numerous exams and achieved certification in specialties of powerplant (engines), hydraulics, electronics, controls and operating systems before becoming crewmembers of their respective aircraft.

Benardini and Seal monitored the control panels each time their plane's engines started up, while taxing and taking off, during flight and while landing. They were able to recognize problems before they developed, simply by observing gauges and meters that provided such information as cylinder-head temperature, oil temperature and pressure, air intake temperature, exhaust temperature, manifold pressure, hydraulic system pressure, and a host of other conditions. The pilot often called the flight engineer over the intercom whenever he needed information about the mechanical or electrical operations aboard the craft.

Problems developed in flight from time to time—some were random and others resulting from combat. Seal and Benardini were on the spot quickly to analyze such problems and determine the best course of action for resolving them. If an overheating engine could be resolved by reducing its power setting, the problem might be managed by adding power to the other three engines. The failing engine might have to be shut down and its propeller feathered—the propeller blades aligned with the airstream in order to reduce drag to a minimum. If hydraulic pressure was seriously low, perhaps due to combat damage, the landing gear might have to be cranked down by hand—a tedious process requiring quite a bit of time. The pilots depended on Seal and Benardini to maintain the aircraft in optimal operational status during flight.

THE RADIOMAN

Sergeants Wayne Simmons and Edward Buffington spent the majority of their home-side training learning the 'ins and outs' of radio and electronics. Their job wasn't simply to tune in and listen to a radio. The radioman sought out radio signals from distant cities, tuned them in and determined the direction to or from those particular radio transmissions. This provided the navigator and pilot with directional components (i.e., *72/288-deg*, *134/226-deg*, etc…). When two such signals were tuned in, a 'fix' could be determined at the point they intersected, thus providing a location for the aircraft. When the radio signals originated close by, the plane's location could be determined fairly accurately, but when the signal originated from a distant transmitter, the plane's location might be a bit less precise.

The radio compass was an important piece of navigational equipment on the bombers. Whenever a breakdown occurred with either the magnetic or gyroscopic compasses, the radio compass provided redundancy in determining direction. The aircraft were also equipped with telegraph equipment consisting of a telegraph key and transmitter. The telegraph unit served for back-up communication but could also be utilized for emergency direction finding.

The bombers had a lot of radio equipment onboard, and it was the subject of frequent breakdown. Simmons and Buffington were responsible not only for operating the various pieces of radio equipment but also for fixing and maintaining them in good operation order. In addition to their duties as radio operators, Buffington and Simmons were trained as gunners. When in combat zones, Simmons took up the nose turret gunner position on his B-24. It was a small, tight compartment atop the forward nose of the aircraft. Once inside, with the doors closed, he rotated the electric-powered turret from side to side while scanning the skies for enemy fighter planes. The twin 50-calibre Browning machine guns where balanced so that little force was required to move them up and down. Buffington's other job was that of armorer on his B-17. Prior to arrival near the target, he went to the bomb storage compartment, removed the lock pins that freed the spinners on the nose of the bombs and prepared them for release. He was assisted by other gunners as needed.

THE GUNNERS

The enlisted men manned 50-calibre Browning machine guns at different places throughout the aircraft. Most stations were equipped with twin guns. The belly-mounted ball turret position was particularly hazardous, especially on the B-17 bomber where it was permanently affixed. The B-24 bomber had a retractable ball turret, allowing the gunner to remain in the aircraft except during periods of attack by enemy fighter planes.

Sgt. Vernon MacNeil, ball turret gunner on the B-24H bomber, the *Shilay-Lee*, had a 360-degree field of view through which to rotate the turret while firing rounds at incoming fighter planes. The Sperry ball turret was kept retracted into the fuselage during take-off and landing; otherwise, it could easily be scraped off, due to the low-slung belly of the B-24. When in the combat zone, MacNeil entered the turret door from within the fuselage after which it was deployed to combat position through an electrically operated hydraulic system. From below, he reported any immediate concerns directly to the pilot through the intercom. His helmet liner contained a pair of built-in headphones, and the strap held a throat microphone through which he spoke. When not in the combat zone, MacNeil moved about the aircraft assisting with one task or another, for there were always things to be done. He kept his parachute stowed in the fuselage near his duty station so he could retract the turret, attach his parachute and make a hasty exit if necessary.

Sgt. Leslie Jensen entered the ball turret from inside the fuselage of the *Hearts and Flowers*, a B-17G bomber. His duties were similar to those of Sgt. MacNeil except for entry and exit from the turret—it was a bit more difficult. For that reason, he remained curled up inside the 44-inch sphere for longer periods of time than did MacNeil. On one occasion, Jensen called over the intercom to advise the pilot, Lt. Leo Bollei, that the right inboard engine was trailing fire and smoke along the underside of the wing. Bollei realized the engine had been hit by gunfire from an FW-190 enemy fighter but was unaware the engine was on fire.

In their curled, fetal-like positions within the ball turrets, Jensen and MacNeil each had a decent field of view between his knees, peering straight down the barrels of a pair of 50-calibre Browning machine guns. The turret could be swiveled around or up and down when tracking enemy fighter planes.

The left and right waist gunners braved hurricane force winds and severe cold while manning their guns. Sgt. Raymond Crouch, left waist gunner on the *Hearts and Flowers*, had to leave his duty station hastily on one occasion but returned to get his insulated right glove—it had frozen onto the handle of the guns. His hand would have frozen within a few seconds had he not retrieved the insulated glove, the air temperature being –20⁰ F. Sgt. Joseph Cutrone, the right waist gunner, received the *Purple Heart* from having been hit by a jagged shard of flak—a fragment from an exploding shell—on one mission. When not in combat, Plexiglas windows covered the openings and made their environment considerably less hostile.

Sgt. Robert Bluhm, right waist gunner on the *Shilay-Lee*, was knocked unconscious by a jagged piece of flak that penetrated his metal helmet, passed through his insulated flight cap and stuck in his skull. Sgt. Vernon MacNeil and Cpl. Douglas Millar came to his rescue while

Sgt. Allen Christianson manned his left waist gunner position, firing off round after round at German fighter planes.

Sgt. Wayne Simmons suffered an injury above his ear by a piece of shrapnel. It never completely healed. Family members suggest the injury may have contributed to his early death.

Tail gunners were physically isolated from the rest of the crew during combat operations. Sgt. Hugh Moore sat in cramped quarters manning twin machine guns, his only contact being through the plane's intercom system. On one occasion when the intercom was knocked out by enemy fire, one of the crew rushed back to inform him of an onboard emergency. In this case, Moore had to climb out of the turret to reach his parachute in the aft part of the fuselage in order to prepare for bailing out. Sgt. Jack Haney was at a greater disadvantage as tail gunner on the *Hearts and Flowers*. Rather than a turret, he was perched on a small seat within a very tight space that allowed very little room for turning his head from side to side. A fast exit from his position wasn't possible, for he had to climb over the seat back and then crawl through the narrow, confined rear part of the tail cone before getting to his parachute. In case of having to bail out of the plane, he then had to crawl over oxygen tanks and other stowed equipment before making his way to the bombay to jump.

The top turret gunner positions were above and just back of the flight deck. In an emergency, Sgt. Wilburn Seal could drop to the flight deck, attach his parachute and make his way to the open bombay quickly. Both he (on the B-17) and Sgt. James Benardini (on the B-24) were often called down to assist the pilot with monitoring various engine, propeller, hydraulic and other operating systems. In-flight problems were frequent, some due to combat and others due to ordinary, random malfunctions.

Sgt. Wayne Simmons occupied the Emerson nose turret of the *Shilay-Lee* when in the combat zone. It was positioned directly above the bombardier's post. Pilots often complained of the nose turret blocking part of their forward field of view, for the dome extended several inches above the forward nose of the B-24H. Access to the nose turret was through two small doors that were closed after Simmons perched on the small padded seat. The inside space was quite confined, although not to the degree as in the ball turrets. Simmons had a wide field of view through which to rotate the turret. Fifty-caliber Browning machine guns were mounted on either side of the turret, providing Simmons with a lethal force of lead aimed at any enemy fighter plane that happened to come within his range. The nose turret was also the most precarious place to be when the aircraft was entering a flak zone, for it faced directly into the oncoming metal shards.

Each crewmember knew where he was supposed to be at any given time and what he was supposed to be doing. Whenever unanticipated changes in assignment became necessary, the pilot issued individual instructions to the crew regarding such assignments.

THE *"SHILAY-LEE"*—OFF TO AFRICA

DECEMBER 1, 1943

- Lt. Francis "Mike" Boyle, pilot
- Lt. Frederick "Sam" Moore, co-pilot
- Lt. Robert Barker, navigator
- Lt. Julius Altvater, bombardier
- Sgt. Wayne Simmons, radioman/nose gunner
- Sgt. Vernon MacNeil, ball turret gunner
- Sgt. Hugh Moore, tail gunner
- Sgt. Robert Bluhm, right waist gunner
- Sgt. James "Moose" Benardini, flight engineer/top turret
- Sgt. Allen Christianson, left waist gunner

On the first of December, the *Shilay-Lee*—#41-29239—in the company of the 727th Squadron, 451ˢᵗ Bomber Group, departed Nebraska, headed for the Army Air Base just outside West Palm Beach, Florida. Seven hours and 1,500 miles later, the frigid cold of Nebraska was exchanged for the tropical warmth of southern Florida. The plane was checked over in great detail, serviced and made ready to head to the war zone. The name *"Shilay-Lee"* was painted on either side of the fuselage just back of the Plexiglas nose. On December 7—the two-year anniversary of the Japanese attack on Pearl Harbor—the crew was roused early, boarded the "*239*" and rumbled down the runway. No one knew where the group was headed but, an hour into the flight, Lt. Boyle opened the sealed orders, came on the intercom and announced the destination to the crew—North Africa.

THE ITINERARY

- Puerto Rico—Borenquin Field
- Trinidad, West Indies—Waller Field
- Belem, Brazil
- Forteleza, Brazil, Adjacento Field
- Dakar, West Africa
- Marrakesh, French Morocco
- Constantine, Tunisia

Most of the crew had never heard of these places, but they understood that they were on the way to the MTO (Mediterranean Theater of Operation). Brief refueling stops were made at designated points along the route, with the plane and crew being 'disinfected' with DDT fog at each stop. At Adjacento Field in Brazil, the plane was thoroughly checked for any required maintenance and repair as the crew prepared for the long hop across the Atlantic to Africa. They had several free days during which to walk on the beaches, visit the area and relax before departure.

On December 23, the *Shilay-Lee* roared down the runway—minus Julius Altvater—circled to gain altitude to around 8,000 feet and set on a heading toward Africa. Altvater had 'caught a bug' and had to remain in Brazil a few days in order to recover. The arrival of the *Shilay-Lee* at Dakar depended on navigator Bob Barker's training and experience, for there were no navigational aids during the ten-hour flight across the open water other than taking a fix on the stars. Barker's calculations were right on target, placing them almost directly on Dakar. The other 'legs' were a snap, and they arrived at Talergma, near Constantine, Tunisia, on Christmas Day. A week later, Altvater arrived on another plane and joined the crew.

Things were not so neat and orderly at Talergma, for the nights were freezing and mud was everywhere. General Erwin Rommel's *Afrika Korps* had been driven out several weeks earlier, leaving the entire area cluttered with leftovers from intense battles that had taken place. The crews slept in tents with dirt floors. The cold nights were tempered with heat coming from homemade barrel stoves. Petrol dripped from a copper tubing onto sand, producing an open flame that provided heat—a most dangerous system! A tent occasionally exploded, causing injuries and bringing down the wrath of superiors.

Airplanes became stuck in the mud and had to be extricated with trucks or whatever machines that could be requisitioned for the job. Special perforated steel panels (PSPs) were laid out across the muddy terrain to form taxiways and runways. Fuel was transported from the nearest ports and was transported in barrels by truck. Dust occasionally swirled so badly that one could barely see the fingers on his outstretched arms. Conditions were primitive. Crewmembers sometimes slept in their planes in order not to have to deal with the dirt and mud, and also to guard against sabotage or theft.

The planes went out daily, weather permitting, preparing man and machine for what lay ahead—war, real war. The planes were kept covered with tarps in order to keep dirt and dust from getting into—and ruining—everything. Engines were especially vulnerable to the existing conditions. After returning from a flight, time had to be allowed for them to cool down before being covered.

Telergma, Tunisia, North Africa; *Front row, L to R*: Boyle, H. Sternberg; *standing*: Bluhm, Simmons, MacNeil

The *Shilay-Lee* took off for Italy on January 10, 1944, in the company of dozens of other B-24 Liberators, with the first station at Gioia de Colle just above the 'boot heel.' Liberators were parked all over the place in preparation for the coming onslaught against the German forces further to the north and east. The site was so close to sea level that high tide sometimes left the ground drenched from sea water. Practice missions were carried out on most days in order to acquaint the crew with upcoming real-life missions. They now operated like a finely tuned machine, with each member well prepared and equipped to carry the war to the enemy.

Conditions at Gioia were quite primitive. Again, the crew slept in tents as they had in Africa—the four officers were in one tent and the six enlisted men in another. It rained a lot, so they often had to trudge around in mud. Runways and taxiways had been scraped out and covered with PSPs to keep the heavy bombers from becoming mired in the mud. Conditions weren't exactly comfortable, but they adapted to the hardships.

The squadron went out on practice formation flights when weather permitted, crossing the Adriatic Sea to the northeast, flying patterns that brought them back to home base. Near the end of the month, they were deemed combat ready so, on January 30, 1944, the 727th Squadron of the 451st Bombardment Group of the 15th Air Force carried out its first mission—a bombing raid on the German radar station at Fier, Albania. And then, things started getting serious—*REALLY* serious!

The procedure for missions always followed the same pattern. Sometimes it was scratched (canceled) because of weather at home base or over the target. If the mission was on, the crews were roused around 4:00 AM. They shaved using cold water—shaving was required to prevent face stubble from interfering with the fur-lined flight helmets. Shortly, they were picked up in open, stake-bed trucks and transported to the mess hall—a tent structure—where they had breakfast. The officers and enlisted men ate separately but were served the same food which was nothing to write home about—hard pancakes, spam, dried reconstituted eggs and coffee, complete with the grounds. This would be their last meal before returning from the day's mission which might be up to ten hours. An oversize plywood panel stood on wooden legs at the 'business' end of the tent; it was draped with a large sheet that covered a big wall map.

"Atten-shun!" It was suddenly quiet as everyone came to order. The wall map was uncovered, and mission procedures were discussed and defined. A red string tacked onto the map at 'home base' was stretched across to the target. Predictions were provided for possible danger from the enemy along the flight path, on the ground and in the air. Potential weather outlook was described. Aircraft formation and individual positions were assigned, headings and flight paths were specified and the mission was set. The pilots and co-pilots remained in the briefing room for special last-minute detailed instructions while the other crewmembers boarded open trucks and were transported to their respective aircraft.

Castelluccio, Italy; tent housing, Simmons' bike

Mention should be made of the Norden bombsight and the bombardier's special responsibilities.

[During World War I, there arose the need for aiming free falling bombs so they would strike the desired target with the highest degree of accuracy. The "guess-and-drop" system gave way to mechanical sights located on the plane whereby the "bombardiers" achieved greater accuracy. During this era, noted engineers worked on design and construction of more sophisticated bombsights for achieving even better accuracy. A Dutch inventor, Carl Norden, developed the most advanced bombsight of the time, and in 1928 it was unveiled to the U.S. military under highest secrecy. Norden had previously worked with Elmer Sperry on gyro stabilizers for various craft. The Norden bombsight was readily adopted and became one of the most carefully guarded secrets over the next twenty years. Sperry also developed an effective bombsight, but the Norden bombsight was the standard for most American bombers.

It was similar in size to that of a common suitcase. It took into account all the physical and mathematical factors for assuring bombs would drop onto the target with highest accuracy. Various controls allowed the bombardier to input (1) aircraft elevation above the terrain, (2) aircraft airspeed, and (3) drift—by combining wind speed and direction. The bombardier depended on the navigator to provide much of the input data.

The Norden bombsight technology was very high tech for its day and was so secret that bombsights were kept locked in secured vaults with military guards present. A special 'master' maintained the keys in another secured vault. There was no way to gain access to the Norden bombsight without proper authorization.

On the day of a mission, the bombardier was escorted to the site by military police, the vault was opened and the Norden bombsight was removed and transferred to the bombardier. It was carried within a black box with a carrying handle on top. The bombardier was escorted to his aircraft, the instrument taken on board, removed from its case and bolted onto its placement within the forward nose of the craft. The only people to actually observe the bombsight were any crewmembers that happened to be in the nose of the aircraft during a mission.

The secrecy of the bombsight was so heavily guarded that the bombardier was responsible for destroying the instrument with an internal explosive device, in the event of an accident or anticipated crash. The technology of the Norden bombsight was not to be divulged in any way to the enemy.

Most who used the Norden bombsight during the war had high praise for it. When operated correctly, it provided the very best and accurate means for delivering bombs to enemy targets. It was constantly upgraded with the aim of improving its performance, several modifications having been made during the course of the war. The Sperry bombsight was employed in some aircraft, but the Norden instrument was the standard for most U.S. Air Force planes during World War II. In actual practice, the bombardier collected all relative information from the pilot and navigator—aircraft airspeed, elevation above the terrain, compound wind speed and direction. He input these factors into the bombsight and visually observed the ground through the binocular optics of the instrument. As the aircraft was nearing the I.P (initial point) of the bomb run, the pilot switched directional control of the plane to the bombardier who then guided the craft along the path toward the A.P. (aiming point), or intended target. A "toggle" lever allowed the bombardier to move the craft slightly left or slightly right in order to maintain the track toward the target as he visually observed the ground path of the aircraft through the view scope. The time between the Initial Point and Aiming Point was usually about six to seven minutes. When the cross-hairs passed directly over the target, the bombardier pressed the bomb release button, dropping the bomb load. Other bombers in the group dropped their bombs,

either mechanically or electronically, on cue from the
lead bombardier, resulting in "carpeting" the area on
top of and around the target.]

The ground crews had the bombers serviced and ready to go by the
time the crews arrived for boarding. Crewmembers came aboard with
their parachutes and other equipment required for the mission. Each
had his own list of pre-flight inspections to complete in order to ensure
that everything was performing according to specifications. The pilot,
copilot and flight engineer did a walk-around of the aircraft, making
visual inspection of the propellers, control surfaces, wheels and tires,
hatches and the exterior to ascertain that everything was in proper
operating condition. After boarding, the control surfaces—elevator,
rudders, ailerons, flaps—were operated through their full ranges of
motion to determine proper operation. The engines coughed and
belched smoke as they were started and allowed to warm up for several
minutes.

Following warm up and instructions from *Ground Control*, the
planes taxied out according to their individually assigned positions,
stopping just short of the end of the runway where the engines were
'run up' to proper rpm and checked for performance. The propellers
were individually run through their cycles at this time. When the order
came from the *Tower*, the next plane in line taxied over to the end of
the runway and aligned its nose with the center stripe. Brakes were set
and power was applied to the four engines, with the propellers set at
minimum pitch and optimum engine rpm for take-off. It was usually
around sun-up by the time the bombers were ready to take off. When the
Tower barked the instruction, "*Cleared for take-off*," brakes were released
and the overloaded behemoth—with full fuel tanks and maximum
bomb load—started its roll down the runway. Acceleration was slow
but, little by little, the huge monster gained momentum. It seemed
like everyone held his breath as the pilot and co-pilot strained forward
in their seats as if to assist the aircraft in lifting off the ground. With
most of the runway behind, and with the other end fast approaching,
the wheels lifted off momentarily, touched again and then lifted off
for good. The pilot held the craft just a few feet off the ground as the
big bomber gained airspeed. The forward wheels were retracted, and

a gradual climb was set up toward the rendezvous with other planes already in the holding pattern and pulling into formation.

If, for example, seventy bombers were scheduled for a mission, the last plane took off about thirty-five minutes after the first plane. The early planes were already climbing into their specific positions within the formation by the time the last plane, dubbed *"Tail-end Charley,"* left the ground. This aircraft was usually the most vulnerable, for the Luftwaffe fighters often attacked from the rear, flying through the formation while firing off as many rounds as possible into the bombers. The bombers couldn't take evasive action until after dumping their bombs on the target, so *Tail-end Charley* often got the worst pounding from the repeated passes of the enemy fighters.

Heavy flight suit worn by crewmen on missions

The B-24 Liberators ordinarily cruised at elevations of four to five miles above the ground where air temperatures were -20⁰ F or lower. Bulky, fur-lined leather clothing was necessary, including boots, headgear and gloves. This attire was less than comfortable, and it restricted the crewmen's physical movements. The *"239"* was equipped with electric flight suits for warmth. Once airborne, the suits were plugged into outlets near the duty stations. Oxygen was required at elevations above ten thousand feet, so oxygen masks covered their faces throughout much of each mission. Parachutes were normally stowed near duty stations. The men were familiar with the procedures for wearing and using them. Once zipped up in high elevation gear, it was next to impossible to take care of bathroom problems.

Security was imperative. Reference altitude for the lead plane was stated but not to be included in the pilots' notes; it had to be memorized. For example, if the reference altitude for a specific mission happened to be 'nineteen thousand feet,' the lead plane in the formation flew at that elevation, and other airplanes flew according to their positions within the formation. At some point along the route, the pilot of the lead plane might radio a message indicating a change to "reference elevation plus four thousand feet," or "reference elevation minus one thousand feet." An enemy who might happen to overhear such message would have no idea as to the exact flight elevation of the formation.

Nearing a target such as a ball bearing factory or an oil depot, the enemy might have a hundred or more 88-mm Howitzer cannons stationed around the site. These guns, considered to be the highest performance guns of the war, were capable of firing large shells as high as thirty thousand feet. The shells were equipped with barometric fuses that could be pre-set to explode at a specific altitude after being fired, with the object of producing clouds of flak fragmentation at the same elevation and flight path of the bombers. The enemy cannons were capable of firing up to twenty shells per minute. A single piece of flak—a metal shard—could knock out an engine, cause major damage to the plane or even kill a crewmember. Flak knocked bombers out of the sky on occasion.

During the approach to the target, a game took place between the bombers and the enemy on the ground. Since last-minute changes in elevation and flight path were limited for big bombers, it was imperative to keep the enemy gunners guessing. At least ten minutes were required to make changes in the fuse settings. If the attacking bombers were able to make changes in elevation a few minutes prior to entering the bomb run, enemy gunners might be caught off guard. If the bombers were lucky, the shells exploded well above or below their flight paths. If the gunners were lucky, the shells exploded directly in the flight paths. Crewmembers knew where to expect heaviest flak by observing the sudden bursts of black smoke where the shells exploded. The bombardier was in control of the plane during the six or seven-minute period leading up to the bomb drop, so straight and level flight was imperative during this period in order to put the bombs on the target with highest accuracy.

The roles of the navigator and bombardier were as important as those of the pilot and co-pilot. Navigator Bob Barker sat in a small area back of the nose section and below the flight deck. His job was to keep the pilot advised of the exact position of the plane at all times. If winds aloft happened to carry the plane to the left of the desired path, Bob would advise the pilot of a needed correction in heading (e.g., "*six degrees to the right*") in order to compensate sufficiently to place the aircraft on the proper flight path. Bob was responsible for navigating the bomber along the correct heading taking the plane directly over the target. Once the bombs were dropped, he provided the headings for getting the plane home safely.

The bombardier, Julius Altvater, had the best viewing position in the plane. From his forward position in the nose, he commanded a wide-angle view of everything ahead and below. He was alone for much of the flight but was joined by Wayne Simmons when the plane was maintaining radio silence—usually an hour or so before reaching the I.P. During periods of radio silence, all crewmembers were in direct communication through the aircraft's intercom system. During radio silence, Simmons moved from the radio compartment to take up position as gunner in the nose turret.

A few minutes before arriving at the I.P., Altvater confirmed that the bombs were 'armed' so they would explode on impact. Arming a bomb consisted of removing the pin that held a small propeller in place on the nose of the bomb. The bombs were further protected from prematurely exploding by a wire threaded vertically through the inertial plunger of each bomb in the column; the wire was attached to the top of the bomb compartment. The plungers were freed, once the bombs dropped from the bombay and accelerated earthward. The airstream spun the propellers, thus 'unscrewing'—unlocking—the firing pins so the bombs would explode on impact. Some types of bombs were fitted with timing devices that resulted in delayed explosion after impact (i.e., ten minutes, thirty minutes, etc...). It was imperative that the planes flew straight and level, and at uniform speed, while approaching the I.P. in order that Altvater could adjust the bombsite accurately.

The distance between the I.P. and A.P. was usually around twenty miles, or about six minutes. Altvater peered into the binocular viewer watching the countryside glide by. He determined the location of the target and aligned it with the plane's flight path. He adjusted the bombsite controls for the exact airspeed of the plane (e.g., *"193 knots"*—about 210 mph), the elevation above the terrain (e.g., *"plus 19,040 feet"*), and the wind drift and ground speed as advised by Barker. At the moment of reaching the I.P., Altvater communicated *"Ready!"* Boyle answered, *"Roger! It's yours!"* as he switched control of the ship to Altvater. The bombay doors were opened. Using the toggle control on the bombsight, Altvater toggled the plane from time to time—slightly left or slightly right—as required to keep it on the exact path to carry it directly over the target. He watched intently, in deep concentration, as the cross-hairs approached the target. At the precise moment of reaching the A.P., he pressed the bomb-release button and yelled, *"Bombs away!"* Sometimes, it was desired to save a few bombs for a repeat pass over the target or for dropping on a target of opportunity during the return flight. The lead bomber of the first element was responsible for leading the entire formation. The lead bomber of each following element keyed off the first (lead) element, and each bomber within an element keyed off the lead bomber of its particular element.

Elements consisted of small groups of planes, usually from the same squadron. The individual elements flew according to their assigned positions within the formation. Individual pilots carefully watched the planes in front and on either side, above and below—flying as closely as possible without bumping into other planes. A tight formation was necessary in order to discourage enemy fighters from penetrating the formation and doing maximum damage. The bombardier of the lead bomber was responsible for coordinating the bomb drop. Bombardiers didn't act on their own but, rather, performed as a team. All bombers in the formation dropped their bombs at the same time, literally carpeting the landscape below. During the latter years of the war, radio devices in the planes were actually networked so that all bombers in the formation were toggled by the lead bombardier, with all bombs dropping simultaneously. The formation was arranged in such a manner that bombs from higher aircraft fell through open spaces within the formation so that a lower bomber didn't get hit by a falling bomb. There were infrequent occasions when turbulence or other factors resulted in a bomber straying from its prescribed position and accidentally getting knocked out of the sky by bombs falling through the formation.

The bomber formation was rarely attacked before nearing the target. Enemy fighter squadrons were based near important sites in order to protect them. They waited on the ground until the bombers were within striking distance before taking off to meet them. This conserved fuel for the enemy aircraft. Once airborne, they climbed rapidly to an elevation of two or three thousand feet above the main body of bombers and off to the side or behind, holding their distance until ready to make coordinated attacks. The attacks ordinarily came from behind or out of the sun. During cloudy conditions, they often lurked behind clouds until the bombers were a half-hour or so from the I.P. at which time they'd sweep in from the rear, usually in the form of a wall, guns ablaze, flying through the formation trying to break it up. The gunners on the bombers fired back at the enemy fighters, shooting some of them down and sending others away trailing smoke. The enemy fighters circled around and made repeated running attacks on the bombers until nearing the target area at which time they kept at a safe distance from the flak zone.

Fighter escort planes accompanied the bombers on nearly all missions. These fighter groups were stationed fairly close to the bomber groups. After the bombers were assembled in formation and on their way, the fighter escort planes took to the skies and caught up with them before enemy fighter planes were encountered. The individual fighter escort aircraft consisted of the P-40 Warhawk, P-47 Thunderbolt, P-38 Lightning and, later, the P-51 Mustang. The P-51 was considered to be the best propeller-driven fighter plane ever produced. The Luftwaffe feared the Mustang more than any other fighter aircraft, for it was more than a match for any plane in their arsenal.

While the B-24 had a range of over two thousand miles, fighter planes were generally limited to around five hundred miles. American fighter aircraft were fitted with aerodynamically designed aluminum drop tanks attached on the underside. Fuel was first consumed from the drop tanks until nearing the combat zone, at which time they were jettisoned, leaving the planes with full fuel tanks for the remainder of the mission. Some fighter planes carried two smaller drop tanks rather than the larger single drop tank. The added fuel extended duration in flight and provided sufficient time for the fighters to escort the bombers into harm's way, fight off enemy fighters and return to base with the bombers after the bomb drop. In addition to its wing tanks, the P-51 was retro-fitted with an extra 80-gallon fuel tank located directly back of the pilot. This adversely affected the weight and balance of the craft, so fuel was consumed from this tank immediately after exhausting fuel from the drop tanks.

Friendly fighter planes rarely flew through the formation, because the gunners on the bombers usually fired at everything that moved. Fighter aircraft, both friendly and enemy, rarely entered the zone where flak was present, but the escort fighters engaged enemy fighter planes anytime they approached the bombers. The P-51 Mustang ruled the skies, once it arrived, experiencing a much higher kill ratio than its predecessors.

Once the bombs were dropped, the bombers circled back toward home as quickly as possible, trying to maintain tight formation so enemy fighter planes couldn't easily fly through the formation and make repeated attacks. Bombers damaged from the bomb run often lost airspeed or elevation, dropped behind and became easy targets for enemy fighter pilots. American fighter planes engaged the enemy during this extremely hazardous period in order to protect the straggling bombers already wounded in battle. The crippled aircraft that managed to make it back home were repaired as swiftly as possible in order that they might return to fight another day. Badly damaged aircraft were sometimes scavenged for parts—engines, control surfaces, landing gear, electronic and other components were transferred to other aircraft needing such hardware.

THE MISSIONS—1944

Combat missions were carried out against targets for which the crew was allowed credit for having completed 'one' mission. During these missions, the aircraft and crew were exposed to enemy combat response ranging from light to moderate intensity. There were other missions, however, during which they were under extremely hazardous conditions—when casualties were anticipated to be in the high percentage category. These were classified as 'double-credit' missions. The *Shilay-Lee* carried out both 'single' and 'double-credit' missions.

During regular combat missions, losses were relatively low; sometimes there were none and at other times there were a few. A group of sixty aircraft would return after having lost two, three, or perhaps five aircraft—well under ten percent loss. These missions included bombing runs made on lightly defended positions such as bridges, radio facilities, seaports, enemy troop concentrations, etc…

Those combat missions carried out to permanent enemy locations— such as oil refineries and depots, aircraft factories, and industrial centers—were heavily fortified with hundreds of heavy artillery pieces and high concentration of fighter planes. American bombers flew through heavy enemy gunfire and dense clouds of flak after having fended off a hundred or more attacking fighter planes in order to reach the target. Losses on these missions were horrendous, sometimes amounting to fifteen or twenty percent of the bombers and crews.

The probability of a particular plane or crewman surviving more than twenty missions was pretty low—around fifty percent. Ninety percent of crewmen didn't survive thirty missions.

The mission summary for the Shilay-Lee is detailed on the following page:

- 'Double-credit' missions are denoted with an "*".
- Headings are given in direct-line "degrees magnetic".
- Sgt. Wayne Simmons's actual combat document is included on the page following the mission summary.

Mission	Date	Target	Heading	Distance	Duration
1	Jan 30	Radar station, Fier, Albania	090/270	140 mi	4:14 hrs
2	Feb 03	Marshalling yds, Arresso, Italy	305/125	325 mi	4:45 hrs
3	Feb 10	Beachhead, Anzio, Italy	282/102	225 mi	4:15 hrs
4	Feb 12	Beachhead, Anzio, Italy	282/102	225 mi	4:15 hrs

5*	Feb 22	Aircraft factory, Regensburg, Ger.	338/158	600 mi	8:30 hrs
6*	Feb 23	Aircraft factory, Steyr, Austria	344/164	560 mi	6:30 hrs
7	Mar 07	Marshalling yds, Florence, Italy	306/126	392 mi	8:00 hrs
8	Mar 11	Submarine pens, Toulon, France	292/112	525 mi	7:30 hrs
9*	Mar 17	Marshalling yds, Vienna, Austria	350/170	560 mi	7:30 hrs
10	Mar 19	Aerodrome, Klagenfurt, Aus.	340/160	460 mi	7:30 hrs
11	Mar 28	Marshalling yds, Mestre, Italy	027/207	440 mi	7:00 hrs
12	Mar 30	Marshalling yds, Sofia, Bulgaria	062/242	342 mi	5:30 hrs
13*	Apr 03	Marshalling yds, Budapest, Hung.	008/188	490 mi	7:30 hrs
14	Apr 12	Marshalling yds, Zagreb, Yug.	360/180	440 mi	5:30 hrs
15	Apr 20	Bridge, Mrsh yd, Ferrara, Italy	330/150	420 mi	5:30 hrs
16*	Apr 23	Aerodrome, Bad Voslau, Rum.	032/272/	640 mi	8:00 hrs
17*	Apr 24	Marshalling yds, Bucharest, Rum.	056/236	505 mi	8:00 hrs
18	Apr 28	Submarine pens, Orbetello, Italy	304/124	360 mi	5:30 hrs
19	Apr 29	Submarine pens, Toulon, France	292/112	525 mi	7:30 hrs
20	Apr 30	Marshalling yds, Alessandra, Italy	310/130	500 mi	7:00 hrs
21	May 02	Seaport, La Spezia, Italy	306/122	330 mi	8:00 hrs
22*	May 05	Ploesti, Rumania	058/302	630 mi	8:00 hrs

```
COMBAT RECORD OF: T/Sgt Ora W.
Simmons, 16191988

Date: Mission: Name of Country: Hours
      Number : Target was Not :Flown

1/30:  1      Pier Rad St Alb   4:15
2/3 :  3     *Arrezzo M/Y It.   6:45
2/10:  5     *Anzio Beachhd.    4:15
2/15:  6     *Anzio Beachhd.    3:30
2/22 8,9a    Regensburg, Germ  8:30
2/23 2,9a    *Starr, Aust        8:40
3/7 : 11     *Florence, Italy  8:00
3/17, 14,14a  Schwect, Aust    7:35
3/11  12     *Toulon, France   7:30
3/19: 16     *Klagenfurt, Germ 7:20
3/28: 18     Mestre, Italy:    7:10
3/30: 20     *Sofia, Hungary   5:30
4/3   22,22a *Budapest, Hung   7:35
4/15 25      *Zagreb, Yugo     5:20
4/20. 30     *Ferrara, Italy   5:30
4/23  32,32a *Bucharest, Rum   8:00
4/24  33,33a *Bucharest, Rum   8:00
4/28: 34     Orbettello, It    8:30
4/29: 35     *Toulon, France   7:30
4/30: 36     *Turin, Italy     7:00
5/2   37     *La Spezia, It    8:00
5/5   38,38a *Ploesti, Rum     8:00

MIA          Ploesti, Rumania

Total Combat Hours:       149:25
Total Combat Missions:        22
Total Combat Sorties:         29
```

HERSCHEL D. MAHON,
Major, Air Corps,
Operations Officer.

Combat Record of Sgt. O. W. Simmons

The *Shilay-Lee* flew twenty-one actual missions and achieved a total credit for twenty-seven combat missions. Although all bombs were delivered to target before its demise on the final mission, no credit was allowed due to the *Shilay-Lee* not having returned to base. The first seven missions were flown out of Gioia, Italy. On March 4, the 451st BG was split, with the 727th Squadron being adopted by the 450th BG and deployed further south to an airfield at Manduria, Italy. On April 5, after completing eight more missions, the 450th BG, including the 727th Squadron, was deployed about a hundred miles west to an airfield near Castelluccio along the coast of southern Italy from where the remaining missions were carried out.

Several missions were started but called back due to deterioration of weather at home or over the target. Crewmembers were sometimes called on to accompany a practice flight for training new airmen. No credit was allowed for training missions. Whenever a mission was scratched, or aborted, no credit allowed. Credit was allowed only when a crew flew to the target, delivered its bombs and returned home.

The primary target for a mission was determined by priority and weather. The weather was often bad along the way, or over the primary target, so a secondary target was often scheduled. If flying conditions were poor in all directions, the day's missions had to be scrubbed. When weather was a non-factor, the primary target took the hit.

High priority targets included enemy aircraft factories, ball bearing factories, industrial centers, petroleum refining complexes, railroad centers (marshalling yards) and other targets of importance to the Nazi war effort.

THE "HEARTS AND FLOWERS"—
OFF TO AFRICA
FEBRUARY 22, 1944

- Lt. John B. Donner, pilot
- Lt. Leo Bollei, co-pilot
- Lt. William F. Karlovitz, navigator
- Lt. Keith R. Winder, bombardier
- Sgt. Wilburn W. Seal, flight engineer/top turret gunner
- Sgt. Raymond Crouch, left waist gunner
- Sgt. Joseph J. Cutrone, right waist gunner
- Sgt. Robert L. Jackson, radio operator
- Sgt. Jack R. Haney, tail gunner
- Sgt. Leslie M. Jensen, ball turret gunner

The first week of November, 1943, the crew joined up at Dyersburg Army Air Base in Tennessee for training together in the B-17F Flying Fortress. A coin flip determined that Donner would be the pilot and Bollei would be the co-pilot. After preliminary flight training, the crew was transferred to MacDill AAF Base in Florida and transitioned to formation flying over the next weeks, compiling about 200 hours flight time in the B-17. Another month was spent at Wright-Patterson AAF Base where the entire 463rd Bombardment Group was assembled. The

463rd BG consisted of four squadrons—the 772nd, 773rd, 774th and 775th—with the crew of the Hearts and Flowers assigned to the 773rd BS. On January 21, 1944, the crew picked up a brand new B-17G (SN: 42-31791) for final training and departed for MacDill Army Air Force Base in Florida a month later. On February 22, 1944, the 463rd BG departed MacDill AAF Base on the first leg of its deployment to Africa. Arriving at Cayenne, French Guiana, 10:15 hours later, they refueled, spent the night and continued to Natal, Brazil, the next day—a flight of 07:15 hours. The following day's hop across the Atlantic put them at Dakar on the extreme west edge of Africa. The longest leg of the trip was a non-stop twelve-hour flight to Tunisia on February 26. It was here that the 463rd BG was incorporated into the 15th Air Force under the command of Maj. General Jimmy Doolittle. Refer to Appendix B—*"U. S. Air Force Bomber Groups and Squadrons"*.

Routine practice flights were made from the Tunisia base during the following weeks and, on March 15, 1944, the 463rd and three other B-17 BGs were moved to Celone Field near Foggia, Italy. Twenty B-24 BGs were stationed at other sites further south. These rudimentary airfields were developed after the German forces had been driven to the north. Following orientation flights over the next couple of weeks, the *Hearts and Flowers* flew its first combat mission—a bombing run on the marshalling yards and other strategic targets around Imotski, Yugoslavia. The "791" now had a leading role in destroying the Nazis and bringing the terrible war to an end.

Living conditions weren't entirely pleasant. The crews' homes were primitive shelters—enlisted men slept on cots in one tent, and the officers occupied another. The nights were especially cold, and it was often rainy. Going from one place to another meant that one usually trudged through slushy mud. Most mornings, they were roused from slumber before 4:00 AM and allowed twenty minutes or so to shave and get dressed before being transported to the mess hall in open stake-bed trucks. The fare consisted of hard pancakes, fried spam, scrambled dehydrated eggs and black coffee—every single day! The officers and enlisted men ate at separate places, but they fared no differently. Casual talk and joke exchanges halted abruptly when the commanding officer barked *"Atten-shun!"* over the intercom. A large sheet was pulled off the big wall map at the front, revealing the day's mission. A red twine stretched between home base and the target to indicate the general flight path for the mission. After preliminary briefing, the enlisted men were transported to their planes to assure everything was in order and ready for the mission. The officers were briefed according to their positions—pilots and co-pilots, navigators and bombardiers. They were the last to arrive on the flight line.

Specific ground crews were assigned to individual aircraft. Ground crews had worked throughout the night, readying their planes for the mission. Maintenance and repairs had begun the previous day, following the return of the planes from its mission. By the time the officers arrived from briefing, engines were ready to be cranked up. The enlisted men had already completed the physical check of their planes and systems, so the pilots had only to check the flight controls and related systems. The bombardier was escorted separately to his aircraft after having retrieved the Norden bombsight from the secured vault. The bombsight was carried in a rectangular black-box about the size of an overstuffed suitcase. Once onboard, it was removed and secured it to its placement in the forward nose of the aircraft. The navigator carried the maps for the mission, along with special tools for taking 'fixes' along the flight path. In the B-17, his duty station was located in a small niche in the forward section of the fuselage. An overhead Plexiglas window provided direct visual access for taking reference 'fixes' from the sky. When requested by the pilot, the navigator could cross the narrow catwalk along the center of the bombay and step up to the flight deck just back of the pilot and co-pilot. When necessary, he could provide assistance to the pilot by navigating directly from the plane's main instrument panel.

The 463rd BG flew missions beginning in March of 1944. A mission usually consisted of a 'wing' (three or four BG). Each BG normally consisted of four bomber squadrons (BS), with each squadron having around fifteen to twenty aircraft. A wing might include up to three hundred aircraft. The actual number of aircraft in a particular squadron varied from week to week, generally depending on battle damages and casualties.

THE MISSIONS

The combat missions flown by the *Hearts and Flowers* included both 'regular' and 'double credit' missions. The crewmen were awarded double credit for those missions that were deemed extremely hazardous—when the aircraft and crew were exposed to extremely high enemy response and when casualties were expected to be high. Missions were designated as 'regular' whenever the enemy response was anticipated to be light to moderate, such as those to seaports, radar stations, bridges and industrial centers. Double credit missions included heavily fortified, high priority sites such as oil refineries and depots, aircraft and ball bearing factories, and railroad and transport centers.

The missions flown by the 463rd BG/773rd BS are listed, including the general magnetic course heading, distance and duration of each flight—from take-off until touch-down. Double credit missions are denoted by the "*" symbol.

MISSIONS FLOWN BY THE 463RD BG

Mission	Date	Target	Heading	Distance	Duration
1	Mar 31	Marshalling yds, Imotski, Yug.	030/210	160 mi	4:45 hrs
2	Apr 02	Marshalling yds, Brod, Yug.	090/270	285 mi	6:00 hrs
3	Apr 03	Marshalling yds, Brod, Yug.	090/270	285 mi	5:00 hrs
4	Apr 06	Marshalling yds, Zagreb, Yug.	360/180	310 mi	7:00 hrs
5*	Apr 13	Bridges, dams, Gyor, Hungary	013/193	460 mi	6:25 hrs
6*	Apr 15	Oil complex, Ploesti, Rum.	065/245	585 mi	8:05 hrs
7	Apr 20	Marshalling yds, Vicenzia, Italy	324/144	350 mi	5:15 hrs
8*	Apr 24	Oil complex, Ploesti, Rum.	065/245	585 mi	7:35 hrs
9	Apr 28	Marshalling yds, Piombino, Italy	282/103	290 mi	5:15 hrs

10	Apr 29	Submarine base, Toulon, France	282/102	500 mi	7:40 hrs
11*	May 05	Oil complex, Ploesti, Rum.	065/245	585 mi	8:00 hrs
12*	May 06	Marshalling yds Brasov, Rum.	060/210	585 mi	7:30 hrs
13*	May 10	Airdrome, Aus. Weiner Neustadt	360/180	530 mi	7:05 hrs
14	May 12	Fortifications, Elba Island, It.	285/105	290 mi	5:10 hrs
15	May 13	Marshalling yds, Trento, Italy	324/144	390 mi	4:30 hrs
16	May 14	Marshalling yds Piacenza, It.	296/116	390 mi	6:10 hrs
17*	May 18	Oil complex, Ploesti, Rum.	065/245	585 mi	X

Following the 7th combat mission on April 10, 1944, Lt. Donner and Sgt. Jackson were re-assigned to another aircraft for some unknown reason. It may have been due to the special need for those particular crewmen as replacements on other aircraft. In any case, Lt. Bollei was moved to the pilot position, Flight Officer Sidney Fisher was assigned to the co-pilot position, and Sgt. Edward Buffington replaced Sgt. Jackson. Lt. Donner's aircraft was shot down over Germany on April 30, 1944, after which he was captured and taken to a German POW camp. His POW unit was moved from place to place over the following year as the Germans retreated back into their 'fatherland'. He was liberated in late May of 1944, following the surrender of Germany on May 6. It was reported that Sgt. Jackson perished when his plane crashed into the Adriatic Sea after being crippled during a bombing mission in the early summer of 1944.

Lt. Bollei stated that…

> *"The crew of the HEARTS AND FLOWERS was fortunate to have avoided serious injuries and/or fatalities during their twenty-two combat missions. Antiaircraft shelling and attacks from fighter planes were brutal, with the plane returning home on many occasions having gaping holes and battered mechanical systems. During the first twenty-one*

combat missions, we suffered only one personal injury when Sgt. Joseph Cutrone, right waist gunner, was hit by a piece of flak that came through the plane. He was appropriately awarded the Purple Heart for his injury. Other than that, there were no flight related injuries of which I'm aware.

"On one occasion in particular, flak and enemy fighter planes seriously disrupted an engine. We held course, dropped our bombs on target and had made a sweeping turn back toward home when the engine was hit by gunfire from an enemy fighter plane. The damaged engine shut down, but the propeller continued to spin (wind-milling), creating serious drag and enormous vibration. The plane was difficult to control. We attempted to feather the propeller (align the blades directly into the wind) in order to both stop the engine rotation and reduce the drag, but to no avail. The vibration got so bad that I thought it was going to shake the plane apart. Control of the propeller pitch (angle of the blades) was dependent on oil pressure, but the engine had lost its oil pressure. I'd been successful in partially feathering the prop, but it was now frozen in the mid-way pitch. The vibration worsened as we continued toward home several hours away. Sgt. Wilburn Seal, the engineer, suggested shooting off the faulty propeller from the top turret gun position. I feared creating an even worse problem. Before any decision could be made, however, the plane shuddered momentarily and the spilling propeller broke free. It fell below the wing and disappeared. It's possible that the propeller broke away after the bearings burned out from lack of oil. Running on three engines, we were able to stay up with the formation and return home safely. Falling behind would have resulted in the enemy attacking us in full force."

Haunting questions remain: Did Sgt. Seal shoot off the faulty propeller from his top turret gun position? Lt. Bollei didn't address that possibility, but it's entirely possible, even probable, that the propeller was shot off.

From Sgt. Seal's perspective as the aircraft's engineer, the propeller was literally shaking the plane apart. There was absolutely nothing he or Lt. Bollei could do from the flight deck. The offending propeller was free-wheeling—running free and inducing tremendous drag—causing the aircraft to be almost impossible to control. It was producing considerable leveraged drag force from its outer position on the wing—pulling the wing reversely in the airstream. The other three engines would have had to be powered up to full throttle in order to compensate for the induced drag. Lt. Bollei would have had to apply opposite aileron force to raise the 'problem wing' and, at the same time, apply opposite rudder force (and some elevator force) just to keep the big aircraft moving straight ahead. It would have been virtually impossible to keep from falling behind the other bombers, considering the combined drag from the problem propeller and the settings of the ailerons, rudder and elevator, even with the three remaining engines set at full throttle.

There were two distinct possibilities: one, the aircraft was going to fall apart very quickly, resulting in total catastrophe; or, two, the aircraft was going to fall behind the main group of bombers and become an easy target for German fighter planes. There was little time remaining.

As Sgt. Seal saw it, the propeller had to be removed quickly and decisively. There was only one way to do it—a burst of his 50-caliber machine guns from the top turret. He had a perfect viewing and firing angle from which to sever the prop from the engine. He was right.

As Lt. Bollei saw it, the machine-gun approach might create a worst case scenario—fragmentation from the bullets might deflect into the wing, control surfaces, fuel or hydraulic systems, or even produce a fire! He was right.

Now, if Sgt. Seal disobeyed the order not to shoot off the faulty propeller, he would be in serious trouble after the plane landed. But, if the propeller simply 'went away' without anyone knowing the cause, perhaps there wouldn't be a problem.

When the 50-caliber machine guns are fired from any place within the aircraft, a distinctive shudder is felt.

The author has some questions. First, why was there a distinctive shudder at the moment the offending propeller separated from the aircraft? Secondly, why did it occur within seconds of Sgt. Seal suggesting that the prop could be shot off? It would only take four or five seconds for him to pop up into the top turret, take aim with his Browning-50s. It would only take a short burst (creating a shudder).

The author has flown on a B-17G and looked straight down the barrels of those Browning 50-caliber machine guns from the top turret—located just three feet behind, and above, the pilot's seat. The propellers are just forward of the flight deck and offer a clear line of sight between the guns and the propeller shaft.

It's entirely possible that Sgt. Seal shot the offending prop off the engine. Seal family members and others have described Wilburn Seal as an individual who never saw a problem as being impossible to solve. He never feared taking a risk in order to achieve a positive result.

Can't you just hear Wilburn Seal—the Texas calf-roper and bareback bronco rider—responding to the question as to whether he shot off that prop? He'd probably smile and reply, *"We'll never know, will we!"*

THE "*SHILAY-LEE*"—LAST TRIP TO PLOESTI

May 5, 1944. The *Shilay-Lee*, aircraft #41-29239, lumbered down the runway at Castelluccio Airfield loaded with over 8,000 lbs of bombs and full fuel tanks. After what seemed like an eternity, the wheels lifted off momentarily, bounced easily on the metal PSP decking and the plane became airborne. Lt. Mike Boyle held the huge craft straight and level for a half-minute or so, just a few feet above the flat terrain, in order to pick up airspeed before beginning the climb out. At around one thousand feet elevation, the "*239*" started a shallow, climbing bank to the left that would put it on a heading out over the Adriatic Sea to the east—the rendezvous area for the bombers on the mission. In the gathering light of the early morning, two hundred bombers found their places in the formation and picked up a heading of 058⁰ toward the primary target of the mission—the huge oil refining complex northwest of Ploesti, Rumania. Ploesti was a high priority target because of the Nazi's heavy dependence on the Rumanian oil supplies. It was the major source of fuel for their tanks, trains, aircraft, ships and other mobile war machinery.

Today's mission would be double credit, for it was one of the highest priority sites for both the Allied Forces and the Nazis. It was often described as the deadliest piece of airspace in the world for, like Berlin, the area was heavily defended by large concentrations of heavy enemy artillery and hundreds of fighter planes stationed nearby.

At 13:00 hrs, Lt. Boyle came over the intercom, *"Okay, Guys, let's get to battle stations; we've got about a half-hour before those Jerrys come in! Let's be ready for 'em!"*

Sgt. Wayne Simmons secured the radio equipment, disconnected his intercom and oxygen lines, connected a portable oxygen tank, donned his metal flight helmet, grabbed his parachute and made his way to the nose. Sgt. Vernon MacNeil performed a similar ritual at the ball turret, curled up inside the 44-inch sphere, and deployed the turret into its downward position below the fuselage. Sgt. Hugh Moore made his way toward the rear of the fuselage, laid his parachute nearby, climbed into the tail turret and closed the door. Sgt. James Benardini climbed up into the top turret. Sergeants Allen Christianson and Robert Bluhm took up their stations at the left and right waist gunner positions, and Cpl. Douglas Millar stationed himself in position to capture pictures over their shoulders. Simmons climbed into the nose turret and closed the doors. The gunners reconnected to the intercom and oxygen systems. Boyle instructed them to 'clear their guns' but cautioned them not to send stray bullets in the direction of friendly aircraft. Everything was suddenly 'as usual' for a while.

Far ahead, the first wave of enemy fighter planes had made frontal attacks on the lead B-17 bombers, putting a few out of commission while losing several of their own planes to machinegun fire from P-51 Mustangs. By the time the *Shilay-Lee* approached the flak zone, the enemy fighters were gone—they were landing and refueling before returning to the skies to intercept the bombers heading back toward Italy. Meanwhile, the P-51s circled away in wait of the bombers leaving the target—and the enemy fighters returning to harass them.

Far back in the pack, Simmons noted the familiar black puffball clouds exploding ahead—directly in their flight path. Fighter planes avoided this zone where thousands of pieces of flak—sharp metal shards—rained down on those who entered. The *Shilay-Lee* had no choice. Its mission was to destroy or seriously cripple the Nazis ability to produce fuel for their war machines. Lt. Julius Altvater, the bombardier, communicated with Lt. Boyle over the intercom, stating that he was ready to take over the directional control of the *Shilay-Lee* as they started the final approach to the target.

The minute–by–minute progression of the mission is chronicled in Chapter 1, "MAY 5, 1944."

Crewmen on nearby aircraft reported what they observed after the *Shilay-Lee* was first hit.

Maj. Clayton E. Evans, 6 May 1944:

> *"On May 5, 1944, Lt. Francis M. Boyle…was flying lead ship of the second element of the lead flight. Directly over the target, his plane was seen to suffer a direct hit from anti-aircraft and to catch afire in the fuselage between the wings. The crew attempted to smother the flames while Lt. Boyle continued with the formation. But they were not successful, and parachutes were seen to open. The general opinion of others who flew was that eight or nine chutes opened before the wings folded up and the plane went down. The approximate location of the crash is 45:15⁰ N–23:50⁰ E."*

!st Lt. John J Kavanaugh:

> *"Lt. Francis M. Boyle was flying aircraft #41-29239, as leader of the second element of the lead flight…Directly over the target, the aircraft was hit by flak and caught on fire, in the fuselage, between the wings. The crew attempted to beat the flames out, but it was impossible, and eight or nine chutes were seen to open before the wings folded and the aircraft went down. I was flying as pilot in the lead ship of the high flight and witnessed the above."*

S/Sgt. Darold B. Farless:

> *"I was the nose turret gunner in the lead ship of the high flight of the formation…Aircraft #41-29239 piloted by 1ˢᵗ Lt. Francis M. Boyle was flying the lead position of the second element of the lead flight. Over the target, the aircraft was hit by flak, and a fire began in the vicinity of the top turret. The crew tried to smother the flames, but*

*without success. I saw eight or nine parachutes before the
wings of the plane folded up and the ship went down."*

Cpl. Douglas Millar, photographer (Note PSP runway decking)

The *Shilay-Lee*, mortally wounded when a direct hit from an 88-mm shell exploded in its midsection shortly before reaching the target, struggled to remain airborne and on course. With a raging inferno in the fuselage, the co-pilot slumped across the control column, the right-waist gunner injured and laying semi-conscious on the floor, and the intercom system dead—by some miracle, the *Shilay-Lee* delivered its bombs on the target! Each man performed heroically, under extreme duress, trying to save the burning plane, tending to the injured, and thinking not of himself but of his crew. Not a man considered leaving the doomed aircraft until ordered to do so just moments before the impending explosion.

The photographs on the following page were taken by photographers on nearby aircraft in the formation, recorded the demise of the *Shilay-Lee*—from shortly after it took the direct hit and explosion in the fuselage until it broke apart and fell earthward. The time between the explosion and the crash was approximately forty minutes. The time range is based on reports from those onboard, from reports of airmen in other bombers and from the physical evidence. It is further confirmed by the distance the *Shilay-Lee* traveled after it was hit until plowing into the earth about twenty miles beyond Craiova. MacNeil and Hugh Moore parachuted to earth a few miles north of Craiova, and Simmons touched down a few minutes later about twenty miles northwest of Craiova. (Note: See Simmons's diary, Chapter 11.)

On previous missions, the formations generally followed a particular heading for an hour or two and then changed heading by 15–20° for the next hour or so before making a 90° right turn onto the bomb run. This type flight plan may have been followed for any number of reasons including trying to confuse the enemy, predicted weather along the flight path, navigational considerations, etc… A major advantage of such approach to target would be a much quicker turn off the target toward home, thus departing enemy resistance in a most timely manner.

Considering the formation was probably on a heading of around 170° (almost due south) on approach to the target, and made a right turn off target to around 260° (almost due west), the *Shilay-Lee* would have covered more than 120 ground miles after being hit. Cruising at 200 mph—covering three and one-third miles per minute—the elapsed time between the direct hit and the crash would have been thirty-nine minutes. Considering the fact that the *Shilay-Lee* probably lost some airspeed during the final minutes of its struggle to stay airborne, it may have remained in the air for a bit over forty minutes.

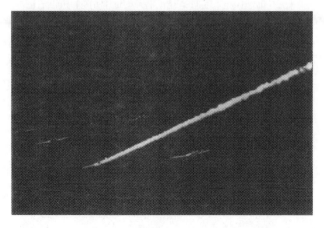

The *Shilay-Lee*, on fire, but holding formation

The *Shilay-Lee*, after breaking apart

Thirteen bombers—ten B-24s and three B-17s —and their crews were lost on this horrific mission. One hundred thirty-four men! (Refer to Appendix C, Bomber Losses on May 5, 1944) For the eleven men aboard the *Shilay-Lee*, the war was over. Lt. Sam Moore, the co-pilot, wouldn't be coming home. He gave his all. Lt. Frances Boyle, the pilot—although mortally injured—stayed with the plane, wrestling at the controls, trying to hold the *Shilay-Lee* in the air long enough for his crew to jump. He succeeded, but the plane exploded before he could bail out. Lt. Boyle paid the ultimate price—his life—in order to save the others.

Lt. Francis "Mike" Boyle, pilot   Lt. Frederick "Sam" Moore, copilot

"Greater Love hath no man than this, that a man lay down his life for his friends." John 15:13

THE "*HEARTS AND FLOWERS*"— FOURTH TRIP TO PLOESTI

May 18, 1944. Well before daylight, 450 heavily loaded bombers took to the skies from airfields scattered around southern Italy. The "*463rd*" BG departed Foggia under less than ideal conditions—heavy clouds and occasional limited visibility—to join other groups assembling over the Adriatic Sea and soon took up a 058⁰ heading toward the primary target—the large oil refining complex northwest of Ploesti, Rumania. At 08:58 hours, the lead group crossed the Yugoslavian shoreline just south of the old walled city of Dubrovnik. Fighter escort soon arrived to accompany the bombers on the mission.

At around 09:20 hours, the weather control center at Foggia made the determination that flight conditions around Ploesti were deteriorating rapidly and that the chances for a successful bombing mission were not good. As Sgt. Leo Bollei put it,

> "*The order went out by radio that the mission was scrubbed and all planes should return to base. Most of the bombers and all of the fighter escort planes picked up the message and returned to their bases, but seventy of the bombers either didn't hear the message or they ignored it and continued toward Ploesti. The Hearts and Flowers was in the lead formation.*"

10:01 hours: The lead bombers crossed from Yugoslavia over into Rumanian territory at an elevation of twenty-two thousand feet.

10:21 hours: The *Hearts and Flowers* passed to the north of Craiova at which time the pilot, Lt. Leo Bollei, ordered the crew to take up duty stations and maintain radio silence until after crossing the target. Crewmembers could, however, still communicate with each other through the plane's internal intercom system.

At 10:22 hours, Sgt. Jack Haney went up to the bombbay, carefully walking along the narrow catwalk while removing the safety pins freeing the nose spinners—arming the bombs— and returned to the tail gunner station. Lt. Keith Winder leaned over the Norden bombsight in the forward nose. A few minutes later, Luftwaffe fighter planes swarmed in to attack the formation, some approaching like "walls" of blazing lightning. With each pass, one or two were shot out of the sky and others drifted away trailing smoke.

The next twenty minutes are chronicled in Chapter 1—"May 18, 1944."

The fighters disappeared as black puff balls of smoke loomed ahead, indicating where 88-millimeter shells exploded. Lt. Bollei described the black smoke as being so thick that it appeared as though one could walk on it. The *Hearts and Flowers* was buffeted and battered by nearby explosions as it plowed on toward the target. Lt. William Karlovitz kept Lt. Bollei constantly apprised of the track, or course, of the *"791"* as they pressed on.

Lt. Winder, the bombardier, advised Lt. Bollei that they were approaching the I.P.—the initial point of the bomb run—and that he was prepared to take directional control of the plane. Lt. Bollei acknowledged and switched control to Winder.

A couple of minutes later, Winder reported: *"Crossing the I.P.!"* He was now steering the plane with the toggle lever on the bombsight. He aligned the cross-hairs in the view scope with the A.P.—the aiming point— and watched the marks tick by as they approached the target.

Six minutes later, *"BOMBS AWAY!"* Winder shouted, at the exact moment they passed directly over the A.P—the presumed target. The huge aircraft lurched upward momentarily as eight thousand lbs of bombs dropped away. The other planes in their group dropped their bombs on cue when they observed the lead plane's bombs fall away, resulting in a carpet pattern of destruction across the target area. Lt. Bollei describes the situation.

"Nearing the target zone and flying at twenty-two thousand feet, we had encountered heavy flak, sometimes so thick you could almost walk on it. But, now, we had a big problem! After dropping our bombs, I couldn't get the bombay doors closed! They were stuck in the open position, creating lots of drag. As we made the wide sweep to head back toward home, we started falling back due to the extra drag. Powering up the engines wasn't sufficient to overcome the extra drag, so we fell further and further back of the formation. We quickly became a prime target for a swarm of about 150 German fighters, mostly Me-109s and FW-190s. They attacked furiously as our gunners poured the lead to them, shooting down several and sending others away—smoking. A FW-190 scored a direct hit into my number-three engine (right side, inboard), setting it on fire. Sgt. Leslie Jensen, the ball turret gunner, reported from below that the engine was on fire and trailing flames near the fuselage (and him, too!). It didn't take long to figure out that the flames were getting too close to the main fuel tank located in the wing—adjacent to the flaming engine. I was in no position to determine the fate of the crew—to permit us to become ten dead heroes. A group of P-38s arrived about this time and chased the enemy fighters away, but it was too late for the Hearts and Flowers.

"I gave the order for everyone to bail out of the ship, that it was going to blow up at any second. I observed them plunge through the open bombay, one at a time, until Sgt. Raymond Crouch turned around and ran back toward the rear of the fuselage. I yelled at him, asking what he was thinking! Crouch replied that he'd left his insulated boots (actually it was an insulated glove) back at his left waist gunner position. He realized that his hand would have frozen almost instantly while falling through the −40° temperatures at our altitude. I watched Crouch return and

jump through the bombay, leaving only myself in the plane. I popped the hatch door, jumped through the opening head first and fell for what I considered to be a long time before pulling the ripcord. When the chute blossomed, however, I found myself at about seventeen thousand feet, drifting downward toward the ground and an uncertain future"

Lt. Leo Bollei, December 7, 2007, at his home in Michigan

Lt. Bollei's gunners put up a valiant last ditch effort during those hellacious twenty minutes, destroying four enemy fighters and sending seven others down trailing smoke before he gave the order for everyone to bail out.

Airmen on nearby bombers described what they witnessed.

2nd Lt. Jules Rose, navigator, 19 May, 1944:

"…B-17G, #42-31791, 18 May 1944…was shot down on bombing raid over Ploesti, Romania…Fighters on full frontal attack, five abreast came in towards Charlie Squadron, then peeled off and followed through in a train past Charlie to Baker Squadron. In the attack Lt. Bollei's ship was hit. He flew in formation for about ten minutes after that. Then he peeled off and passed under Charlie… chutes bailing out all the time. I counted nine chutes and

called to the ball turret who saw the tenth chute...The position was about 10 miles from the Danube River."

S/Sgt. William Marshman, right waist gunner, 19 May, 1944:

"...B-17G, AAF Serial No 42-31791, 18 May 1944... shot down...over Ploesti, Romania. The ship left formation to the right...flying straight and level but drifting out and at a lower altitude. While the ship was in this position both our crew and myself counted five parachutes fully opened and one jump that could have been a long delay. The ship in the meantime, took a course that would have brought it over the Danube River. It was still flying straight and level but losing altitude at the time. Enemy fighters did not seem to bother the ship after it was first crippled."

S/Sgt. Gregory S. Mangin, tail gunner, 19 May 1944:

"...B-17G...No 42-31791, 18 May 1944...over Ploesti, Romania. About ten minutes after the running fight with the fighters was under way. Lt. Bollei's ship peeled off to the right and went down into a glide. Chutes started to come out but it was impossible to follow them any longer due to continuous fighter attacks. I saw about seven or eight chutes open."

S/Sgt. Edward W. Walker, ball turret gunner, 19 May 1944:

"B-17G...Serial No 42-31791, 18 May 1944...shot down over Ploesti, Romania. Ship 791 was behind us about seven o'clock. He was apparently crippled as he was lagging behind. He peeled off with the ship well under control. This took place about 10 minutes after the fight. About this time we saw chutes coming out of the ship. I counted about 8 or 9 chutes. The plane was in a gradual glide headed toward the ground. I did not see it crash."

S/Sgt. Charles E. Hastings, ball turret gunner, 19 May 1944:

"B-17-G...Serial No 42-31791...shot down in raid over Ploesti...I could see him along the trip until we got over the target. He would fall back a ways and then pull up into position. This happened a couple of times but the last time he pulled off to the right and went on a bit farther (then) I saw one chute and a couple of seconds later two more opened. The fighters were coming in continuously so I couldn't watch them very long at a time. I never saw any fire or an explosion."

S/Sgt. Blonnie West, tail gunner, 19 May, 1944:

"Ap B-17G...No 42-31791, 18 May 1944...shot down over Ploesti, Romania. The airplane started drifting to my side of the formation and went into a 360⁰ turn at seven o'clock. It was then I noticed three parachutes blossom. The ship flew a short distance, apparently on automatic control. Then one more chute opened and the ship still flew for a minute before going into a steep glide. It was then I lost sight of the ship as it plunged earthward."

Sgt. Wilburn W. Seal, flight engineer and top turret gunner

As Woody Crouch, Sgt. Crouch's son, described it many years later,

"Initially, when Pappy was about to jump with all the others, he realized that he had left one of his gloves on his Browning-50. If he'd gone ahead and jumped, his hand would have frozen due to the very low temperatures at that high altitude. He thus had to run back in the aircraft to his duty station at the left waist and retrieve it before he could bail out.

"Okay, now, he finally got to bail out and all went well. His chute opened perfectly, and he didn't get strafed by any of "Goring's Boys" in the 109s. But, when he landed in a plowed field near some peasants, he broke his ankle on impact.

"The area farmers, who were armed with shovels, hoes, pitchforks, and scythes, descended on him like he was Frankenstein's Monster and they were the Transylvanian Mob. I'm sure glad it was Romania and not Albania (or was it Bulgaria where they threw petrol and burning matches on parachuting aviators?). As soon as the farmers realized that Pappy actually was injured and essentially helpless and harmless, they backed off and acted pretty nice. He was loaded into the back of a farm cart (horse drawn, I believe) and hauled in to a railroad station. While he was in transit to the railroad, the farmers could tell that Pappy really was in bad pain due to his seriously fractured ankle. For that reason, they decided to treat him like one of their own and applied a very appropriate 'down-on-the-farm' medical treatment. In other words, they fed him very liberal amounts of homemade brandy (apple, or plum)! As I recall, it was described to me as having been of similar potency to the prime corn squeezings made deep in the hills and hollers of Arkansas, Kentucky, and Tennessee. Put simply, it would have burned all night with a bright blue flame and/or peeled the paint off a Tin Lizzie! By the time he reached the train, Pappy was not in nearly so much pain. The data after that is hazy from then until after he arrived at the POW camp."

Sgt. Raymond Crouch, left waist gunner

Picking up the action, Lt. Bollei stated,

> *"Upon landing, a group of Rumanian country people descended on me immediately, brandishing pitchforks and other weapons. I had a 45-caliber pistol strapped to my belt, but there were just too many of them. I quickly surrendered, smiled and handed my pistol over to one of the men."*

Except for Sgt. Crouch's broken ankle, the six enlisted men were quite fortunate to have arrived at Bucharest without any loss of life. They were held in a schoolhouse in downtown Bucharest a few days, interrogated and later transferred to the old abandoned hospital POW camp a couple of blocks from the railroad station and marshalling yards.

Sixteen bombers—nine B-24s and seven B-17s—were lost on this fateful mission. One hundred sixty-five men! Refer to Appendix C, Bomber Losses on May 18, 1944.

BUCHAREST

"There's no place like HOME, and Bucharest sure ain't my home!"

The officers and enlisted men were held separately at the German POW camps around Bucharest, Rumania. The officers were scattered around in a number of different holding places and generally fared better than the others. The Germans considered 'officers' to have 'status'—to be more deserving than enlisted men. The large majority of enlisted men were eventually taken to an old abandoned hospital—a large concrete structure a couple of blocks from the rail center and marshalling yards.

Lt. Leo Bollei describes his greeting party:

> *"They escorted me to an old school building where other men were being held, but I wasn't there very long. They took me to another site where officers were held separately from the enlisted men.*
>
> *"I can understand why those Rumanian countrymen were so upset with American airmen. The Germans had thoroughly indoctrinated them into believing that the airmen were dangerous thugs and criminals hired to fly the planes bombing their country. They didn't know that we were ordinary citizens fighting for our liberty—and theirs."*

Woody Crouch describes his father's experience shortly after Sgt. Crouch's arrival at Bucharest—within a couple of days following his capture:

"The guards took him to an office where Pappy was stood before a German Captain who was seated at a desk or table. The guards stayed beside or behind him. Pappy said he had no idea what to expect, considering all that he had heard about how Nazis interrogated people. This Captain was described as looking like he could have posed for a Nazi recruiting poster—a large blonde Aryan-Nordic man. The Captain studied Pappy for a few minutes and then pointed for him to be seated in a chair. This Nazi then tossed a deck of smokes—Luckies or Camels— and a Zippo on the desk and told Pappy, in totally American English, to light up. Let's just say that Pappy was totally floored by that and especially by what came next. This German Nazi Captain told Pappy that he was originally from America and that he had grown up in a German speaking family who lived near Chicago, Illinois. In fact, he said that he graduated from school in the Chicago area. Pappy said that they had even been to some of the same night clubs in Calumet City! This Captain believed in the National Socialist Party, so he moved to Germany to fight for "The Fatherland" before the (Japanese) attack on Pearl Harbor. A real mind blower is the fact that the Captain told Pappy that he had a brother who was a sergeant in the Army fighting in the Pacific. The Captain and Pappy talked for some time about what apparently amounted to trivia. Then, Pappy was taken back to lock-up. I don't think Pappy ever saw that Captain again; if he did, he didn't tell me about it. According to Pappy, he was not unduly questioned or subjected to anything really bad. I guess this German Captain just wanted to talk with someone who knew Chicago.

"Pappy's comments about the Romanian guards were relatively positive. From what I recall, he said that they were neither cruel nor sadistic and, that under the circumstances, they treated prisoners relatively well.

I seem to recall him saying that the guards were pretty poorly equipped and attired. From what Pappy said, the worst treatment that they suffered in the camp was being subjected to poor quality, inadequate food. I also think that he said that the Rumanian guards didn't eat much better than the prisoners."

Lt. Leo Bollei describes his arrival in Bucharest:

"I was escorted to an old school building where other airmen were being held, but I wasn't there very long. They took me to another site where officers were held separately from the enlisted men.

"I didn't see or hear about any of the other crewmen until after we were repatriated. I was pretty sure all had survived and were in POW camps at one location or another.

"They didn't treat us too badly at the POW camps. Three of us even escaped for a time. Leslie Jensen, Sidney Fisher and I were in the kitchen late one night when we just decided to walk out and see if we could make it to Turkey, 150 miles away. Our biggest worry was getting across the Danube River; so we just walked. About the third day out, we were getting pretty bold, walking through some little village, when they picked us up and took us back to the camp.

"I didn't see or hear anything about the other airmen until after we were repatriated. I was pretty sure all had survived and were being held in POW camps at one place or another."

On reaching the ground—after being blown out of the skies twenty-two thousand feet above Rumania—Sgt. Wilburn Seal floated to earth southwest of Bucharest, near the town of Alexandra. He was promptly captured by local peasants, taken to a military garrison and later transported to the old hospital building that became his POW home for the next several months. It was here that he learned the receiving end of the bombing game. The Americans, British, and Russians frequently bombed the railroad marshalling yards just a couple of blocks away, and the Germans dive-bombed the hospital area because they knew American POWs were interned there. He reported being blown out through a window—twice—by bomb concussion!

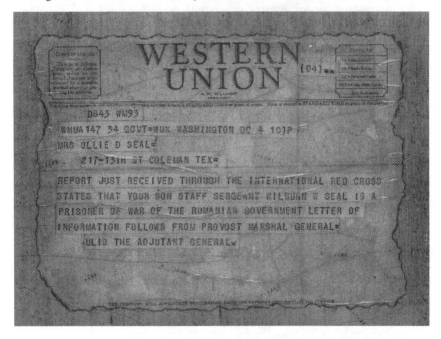

Telegram received by parents of Sgt. Wilburn W. Seal

Sgt. Seal reported in a message sent through the Red Cross from his POW camp in Bucharest that they were treated well but didn't have the quality of food they'd enjoyed back in the military camps in Italy and the U.S. He said the Rumanians were kind but could offer nothing better than soup and sour bread. He told his parents not to worry and that he hoped to be home soon.

Seal described the living conditions as being pretty bad. Several men were crowded into a tiny room having lice-infested beds. He and most of the men slept on the floor, rather than the mattresses.

Fortunately for Sgt. Seal, he'd jumped from the bomber with his full uniform on, and the weather was neither too hot nor too cold. Other prisoners weren't so lucky, for many had no shoes.

Sgt. Robert Bluhm's hometown newspaper reported,

"Sgt. Bluhm was hit in the head and above the eye by shrapnel when his bomber was struck by anti-aircraft fire. Bluhm was rendered unconscious and, when the 'bail out' order came, he was pushed from the plane by the crew. He regained consciousness long enough to pull the rip cord on his parachute and again became unconscious until attempts of Rumanian peasants to revive him succeeded. He was taken in hand by three German soldiers who made him run until they found a cart in which they could haul him to the hospital. After ten days in the hospital, he was taken to the prison camp in Bucharest.

"'The treatment given prisoners left much to be desired,' he commented. They had very few and sometimes no medical supplies during the month and a half he was hospitalized. 'I received fresh dressings for my head wounds only once. They are very inexperienced and far behind in their treatment of many cases, especially those with burns.'

"Daily food ration consisted of one thin slice of black bread for breakfast, a bowl of soup for dinner, and another bowl of soup for supper. 'The soup,' Bluhm said, 'is prepared from some available vegetable, usually cabbage or beans.'

"'The area where we were interned was right in the heart of the Rumanian city with military targets located all around,' he recalled. 'The Americans bombed the area regularly, eight times a month, and the British bombed it eight times a month. We had no air raid shelters, so we had to take refuge under our beds.'"

"Sgt. Bluhm has been awarded the Air Medal with three Oak Leaf Clusters, two presidential citations, the Purple Heart, and the Campaign Medal with two battle stars."

After spending a comfortable night in the country home of one of his captors, Sgt. Wayne Simmons—cousin of Sgt. Wilburn Seal—was taken to a small village in an oxcart where he met up with Sergeants Hugh Moore and Vernon MacNeil. They were taken to Craiova and interrogated, then transported to Bucharest and placed in a military garrison. The following day, they were transferred to a schoolhouse in the center of the city where they remained for the next two months. On July 9, they were moved to the old hospital building where most of the American POWs were interned.

Simmons recorded in his diary the events of May 5, 1944, up until his release from the POW camp. The actual pages of his diary appear, following the text. These are the words of a young man—a boy—not yet out of high school—describing life and death events, not knowing whether each breath might be his last.

Text of Simmons' diary:

"May 5, 1944: We took off at 10:30 AM and crossed the Adriatic, headed for Ploesti. We got across Yugoslavia okay and then we were really looking for enemy planes, but we didn't see any all the way to the target. We were the lead group of the last wave...flying number-four position, and that is an excellent place to be in case the group is attacked. We came to the I.P. (initial point), and flak started bursting all around us, thicker and heavier than I had ever seen before in all my missions, and that was my twenty-ninth one. As we got closer to the target, the flak got heavier and more accurate, and you could feel the shrapnel hitting the ship. We dropped our bombs at 2:35 PM and turned off the target, the flak kept on coming, and then I heard something hit the ship. It sounded like it was tearing it apart. And then I looked around at number-three and number-four engines. Number-three was feathered and the right landing gear was down, but that didn't bother me Then, I saw a FW-190 come under us and take a pass at a ship in our low flight, but he left and I didn't see him again.

"In about a minute, my navigator, Lt. R. J. Barker, opened my turret doors and asked me if I wanted my chute. I told him "No," and he told me he was going up to the flight deck to do his navigating, that all his instruments were shot out in the nose. I told him to go ahead and for him to let me know if things went wrong. I shut my turret doors and sat there searching the sky for fighters and

thinking of how high the smoke was over the target. We were flying at nineteen thousand feet, and the smoke was higher than we were. Then my bombardier opens my turret doors and tells me to get ready to jump. I got out of the turret and got ready, but I didn't think I would have to jump, but I didn't know the ship was on fire. I went back to the bombays and looked up on the flight deck and saw Lt. Moore, our co-pilot, lying on the floor dead and our pilot, Lt. F. M. Boyle, shot in the arm but still flying the ship and doing a good job at it.

"After looking at the fire and seeing it was impossible to put out, the bombardier told me to jump, so out I went. It was really (a thing)! I went down a good way and then pulled my ripcord, and my chute streamed out in kind of a streamer and then popped open. But to my surprise, it didn't jerk me a bit. There I was, hanging in a parachute, about sixteen thousand feet above Rumania.

"I looked up when I heard an explosion and saw our ship in the distance, and the top seemed to be flying off of it, but she was still heading west. There were two more chutes between the ship and (me). I didn't know who they were, but I knew that they were on my crew.

"I seemed to be hanging still in the sky but, when I got closer to the ground, I saw that I was going pretty fast. Then, I saw some peasants running to where I was going to hit. But when I hit the ground, I rolled up my parachute and put it under my arm and started running and looking for a place to hide my chute and myself. I looked back and saw the peasants coming after me, so I dropped my chute and tried to outrun them. I would have if I had been in good shape and if peasants hadn't come from the other way and headed me off.

"There I was, surrounded by Rumanians, about twenty miles northwest of Craiova. The peasants were afraid of me at first but, when they saw that I didn't have a gun, they came up to me and took me to a town a mile north of where I hit the ground. The people were really nice to me. They fed

*me all the fried eggs and beef steak I could eat for supper,
and I had a nice bed that night. But, I was guarded and
couldn't sleep for thinking of what happened to the rest of
the crew. I was hoping they had gotten to Yugoslavia or
had gotten away. I was disgusted with myself for getting
caught, but I found out the next morning that two more
of the guys had been caught. I had fried eggs and rabbit
for breakfast, and then they took me to a small town in an
ox-cart and there I met S/Sgt. Moore and S/Sgt. MacNeil,
two of the boys on my crew. We were taken to 'BA2-S' and
interrogated and sent on to Bucharest and put in a garrison
for one day and then sent to a schoolhouse near the center
of town. We stayed there from the ninth of May until the
ninth of July. Then we were moved to an (abandoned)
hospital in the north part of town.*

*"July 28: I think we are lucky to be here. It is a nice place,
but we are just a block from the marshalling yards. The
15th Air Force comes over almost every day, and we have
been bombed a few times. It is July 28th, and we have been
bombed 45 times. Our building has been hit only twice,
so that isn't too bad. I guess things go along pretty good, all
except the bed bugs; and the food is no good—two bowls of
soup a day and two slices of bread. The lice, crabs and bed
bugs are about to eat us up. I am covered with them.*

*"August 23, 10:45 PM. The Rumanians surrendered to
the Russians, so we are free; but we don't know where to
go or what to do, so we go in the prison camp that night.
We were up early the next morning and walking around,
but the Germans started bombing us, so we ran to an air
raid shelter. The Germans started dive-bombing the air
raid shelter. It was a ten-story building, and I was on
the second floor; so I figured I was pretty safe. But one
bomb came down through the skylight and exploded on
the opposite side of the second floor I was on. It killed over
a hundred people. I don't think any of the American boys
were over there, because two other boys and myself went*

over there, and all the people we could tell anything about were Rumanians.

"We left the shelter and started back to the ex-prison camp. We were about half-way there when the Germans flew toward the running POWs and opened up on them with their guns killing as many as possible. I jumped into a ditch for cover. When the planes left, I found one of my fellow POWs dead only a few feet from the ditch...I feel very lucky to be alive."

The actual pages from Sgt. Wayne Simmons's diary follow:

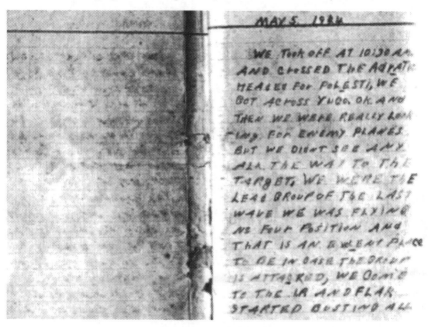

Simmons Diary, a

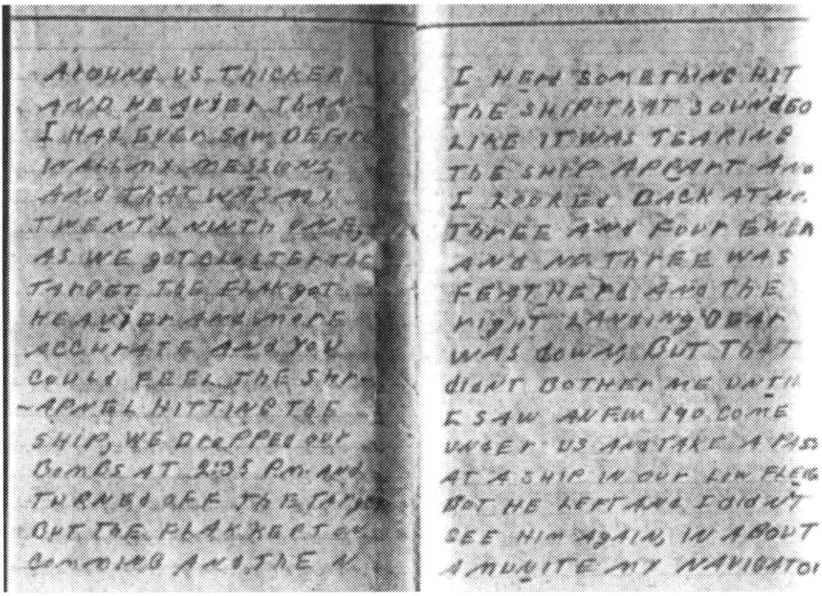

AROUND US THICKER
AND HEAVIER THAN
I HAD EVER SAW BEFORE
IN ALL MY MISSIONS
AND THAT WAS MY
TWENTY NINTH RAID
AS WE GOT CLOSER TO THE
TARGET THE FLAK GOT
HEAVIER AND MORE
ACCURATE AND YOU
COULD FEEL THE SHR-
APNEL HITTING THE
SHIP, WE DROPPED OUR
BOMBS AT 2:35 P.M. AND
TURNED OFF THE TARGET
BUT THE FLAK KEPT ON
COMING AND THE N

I HERD SOMETHING HIT
THE SHIP THAT SOUNDED
LIKE IT WAS TEARING
THE SHIP APPART AND
I LOOKED BACK AT NO.
THREE AND FOUR ENGIN
AND NO. THREE WAS
FEATHERED AND THE
RIGHT LANDING GEAR
WAS DOWN, BUT THAT
DIDNT BOTHER ME UNTIL
I SAW AN FW 190 COME
UNDER US AND TAKE A PASS
AT A SHIP IN OUR LOW FLEIGHT
BUT HE LEFT AND I DIDNT
SEE HIM AGAIN, IN ABOUT
A MINUTE MY NAVIGATOR

Simmons Diary, b

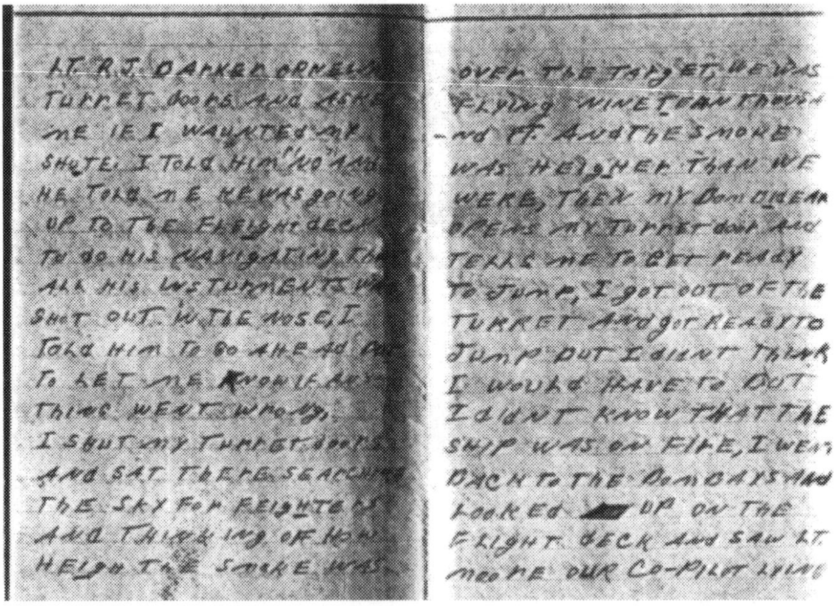

LT. R.J. BAKER OPENED MY
TURRET DOORS AND ASKED
ME IF I WANTED MY
SHUTE. I TOLD HIM "NO" AND
HE TOLD ME HE WAS GOING
UP TO THE FLIGHT DECK
TO DO HIS NAVIGATING, THAT
ALL HIS INSTRUMENTS WAS
SHOT OUT IN THE NOSE. I
TOLD HIM TO GO AHEAD AND
TO LET ME KNOW IF ANY-
THING WENT WRONG.
I SHUT MY TURRET DOORS
AND SAT THERE SEARCHING
THE SKY FOR FEIGHTERS
AND THINKING OF HOME.
HEIGHT THE SMOKE WAS

OVER THE TARGET, WE WAS
FLYING NINETEEN THOUS-
AND FT. AND THE SMOKE
WAS HEIGHER THAN WE
WERE, THEN MY BOMBARDIER
OPENS MY TURRET DOOR AND
TELLS ME TO GET READY
TO JUMP, I GOT OUT OF THE
TURRET AND GOT READY TO
JUMP BUT I DIDNT THINK
I WOULD HAVE TO. BUT
I DIDNT KNOW THAT THE
SHIP WAS ON FIRE, I WENT
BACK TO THE BOMBAYS AND
LOOKED [redacted] UP ON THE
FLIGHT DECK AND SAW LT.
MOORE OUR CO-PILOT LYING

Simmons Diary, c

ON THE PILOT DEAD AND
OUR PILOT LT. F.M. DOVE
SHOT IN THE ARM BUT
STILL FLYING THE SHIP
AND DOING A GOOD JOB OF
IT. AFTER LOOKING AT THE
FIRE AND SEEING IF WAS
IMPOSSIBLE TO PUT IT OUT
THE BOMBADEER TOLD ME
TO JUMP SO OUT I WENT
AND IT WAS REALLY A THING
I WENT DOWN ABOUT
AND THEN PULLED MY
CORD AND MY CHUTE STR-
EAMED OUT IN KIND OF
STREAMER THEN POPPED
OPEN. BUT TO MY SURPRISE

IT DIDNT JERK ME A
BIT, THERE I WAS HANG
-ING ON A PARACHUTE ABOUT
SIXTEEN THOUSAND FEET
ABOVE RUMANIA, I LOCK
-ED UP WHEN I HERD AN
EXPLOSION AND SAW OUR
SHIP IN THE DISTANCE
AND THE TOP SEAMED
TO BE FLYING OFF OF IT.
BUT SHE WAS STILL HEAD-
-ING WEST, THERE WAS
TWO MORE CHUTES
BETWEEN THE SHIP AN
I, I DIDNT KNOW WHO THEY
WERE BUT I KNEW THA
THEY WERE ON MY CREW

Simmons Diary, d

I SEEMED TO BE HANG
-ING STILL IN THE SKY
BUT WHEN I GOT PRETTY
CLOST TO THE GROUND
SAW THAT I WAS COMING DOWN
PRETTY FAST AND STILL
SAW SOME PESANTS
TO WHERE I WAS GOING TO
HIT BUT WHEN I HIT THE
GROUND I ROLLED UP MY
CHUTE AND PUT IT UNDER
MY ARM AND STARTED
RUNNING AND LOOKING FOR
A PLACE TO HIDE MYSELF
AND MYSELF AS WELL BUT
I LOOKED BACK AND SAW
THE PESANTS COMMING

AFTER ME SO I DRIPPED
MY CHUTE AND TRIED
TO OUT RUN THEM AND
WOULD HAVE HAD I
BEEN IN GOOD SHAPE
AND IF PESANTS HADNT
CAME FROM THE OTHER
WAY AND HEADED ME OFF
THERE I WAS SUPPOSED
BY RUMANIANS ABOUT
TWENTY MILES NORTH WEST
OF CRIOVA, THE PESANTS
WAS AFRAID OF ME AT FIRST
BUT WHEN THEY SAW I
DIDNT HAVE A GUN THEY
CAME UP TO ME AND
TOOK ME TO A TOWN

Simmons Diary, e

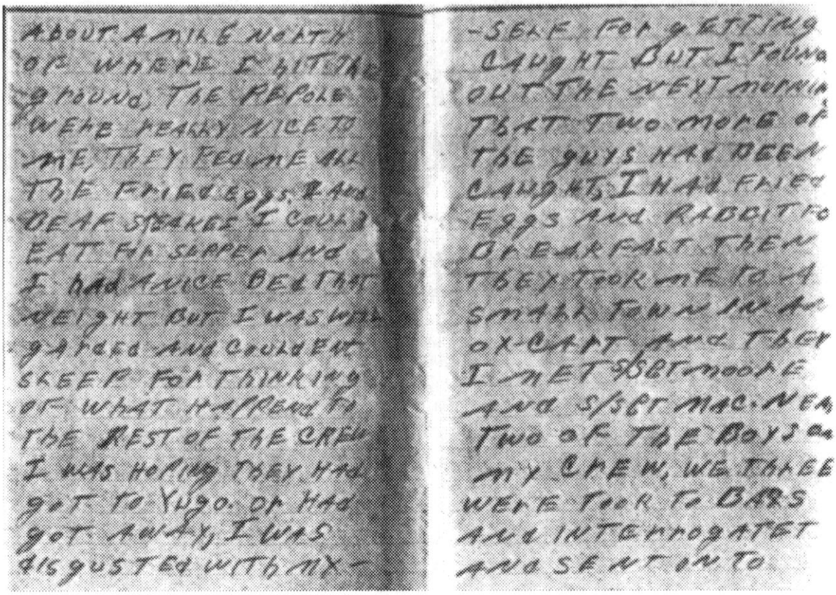

ABOUT A MILE NORTH
OF WHERE I HIT THE
GROUND, THE PEOPLE
WERE REALLY NICE TO
ME, THEY FED ME ALL
THE FRIED EGGS, AND
DEAR STEAKEE I COULD
EAT FOR SUPPER AND
I HAD A NICE BED THAT
NEIGHT BUT I WAS WORR-
-GATED AND COULDENT
SLEEP FOR THINKING
OF WHAT HAPPEND TO
THE REST OF THE CREW
I WAS HOPING THEY HAD
GOT TO YUGO. OR HAD
GOT AWAY, I WAS
DISGUSTED WITH MY-
-SELF FOR GETTING
CAUGHT BUT I FOUND
OUT THE NEXT MORNING
THAT TWO MORE OF
THE GUYS HAD BEEN
CAUGHT, I HAD FRIED
EGGS AND RABBIT FOR
BREAKFAST THEN
THEY TOOK ME TO A
SMALL TOWN IN AN
OX-CART AND THEY
I MET S/SGT MOORE
AND S/SGT MAC-NEAL
TWO OF THE BOYS ON
MY CREW, WE THREE
WERE TOOK TO BARS
AND INTERROGATED
AND SENT ON TO

Simmons Diary, f

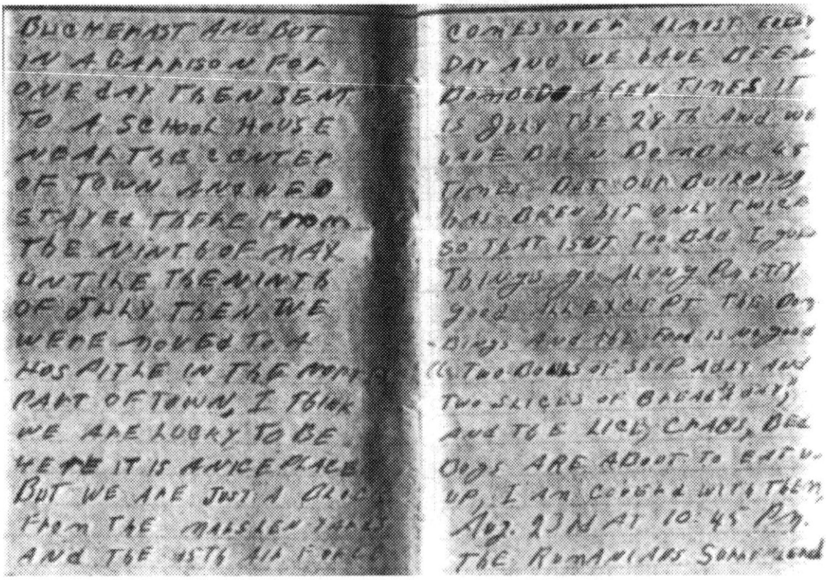

BUCHAREST AND PUT
IN A GARRISON FOR
ONE DAY THEN SENT
TO A SCHOOL HOUSE
NEAR THE CENTER
OF TOWN AND WE
STAYED THERE FROM
THE NINTH OF MAY
UNTIL THE NINTH
OF JULY THEN WE
WERE MOVED TO A
HOSPITLE IN THE NORTH
PART OF TOWN, I THINK
WE ARE LUCKY TO BE
HERE IT IS A NICE PLACE
BUT WE ARE JUST A BLOCK
FROM THE MARSHALLING YARDS
AND THE 15TH AIR FORCE
COMES OVER ALMOST EVERY
DAY AND WE HAVE BEEN
BOMBED A FEW TIMES IT
IS JULY THE 28TH AND WE
HAVE BEEN BOMBED 45
TIMES BUT OUR BUILDING
HAS BEEN HIT ONLY TWICE
SO THAT ISNT TOO BAD I GUESS
THINGS GO ALONG PRETTY
GOOD ALL EXCEPT THE BED
-BUGS AND THE FOOD IS MOSTLY
(2) TWO BOWLS OF SOUP A DAY AND
TWO SLICES OF BREAD A DAY,
AND THE LICE, CRABS, BED
BUGS ARE ABOUT TO EAT US
UP, I AM COVERED WITH THEM,
AUG. 23RD AT 10:45 PM.
THE ROMANIANS SURRENDERED

Simmons Diary, g

TO THE RUSSIANS. SO WE
ARE FREE BUT WE DON'T
KNOW WHERE TO GO OR
WHAT TO DO SO WE
IN THE PRISON CAMP
THAT WE WENT BUT
WERE UP EARLY TH
NEXT MORNING AN
WALKING AROUND
THE GERMANS STA
BOMBING US SO WE
RAN TO AN AIR RAI
SHELTER AN THE G
STARTED DIVE BOMBING T
SHELTER IT WAS A TEN S
BUILDING AND I WAS ON THE
SECOND FLOOR SO I FIGURE
I WAS PRETTY SAFE BUT

ONE BOMB CAME DOWN
THROUGH THE SKYLIGHT AND
EXPLODED ON THE OPSIDE
SIDE OF THE SECOND FLOOR
I WAS ON, IT KILLED ONE
HUNDRED PEOPLE. I DON'T
THINK ANY OF THE AMER-
ICAN BOYS WERE OVER
THERE BECAUSE TWO OTHER
BOYS AND MYSELF WENT
OVER THERE AND ALL THE
PEOPLE WE COULD TELL
ANYTHING ABOUT WERE
ROMANIANS. WE LEFT THE
SHELTER AND STARTED
BACK TO THE EX-PRISON
CAMP. WE WERE ABOUT
HALF WAY THERE WHEN

Simmons Diary, h

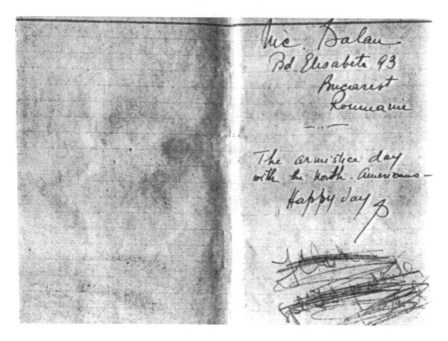

Simmons Diary, j

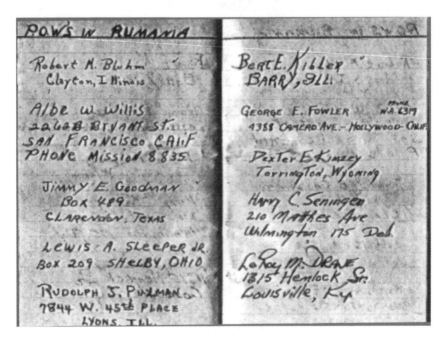

Simmons Diary, k

POWS IN RUMANIA

Robert M. Bluhm
Clayton, Illinois

Albe W. Willis
2262B Bryant St.
San Francisco Calif
Phone Mission 8.835.

Jimmy E. Goodman
Box 489
Clarendon, Texas

Lewis. A. Sleeper Jr.
Box 209 Shelby, Ohio.

Rudolph J. Pulman
7844 W. 45th Place
Lyons Ill.

Bert E. Killer
Barry, Ill.

George E. Fowler   PHONE N.A. 6317
4358 Camero Ave.- Hollywood- Calif

Dexter E. Kinzey
Torrington, Wyoming

Harry C Seninger
210 Matthes Ave.
Wilmington 175 Del.

LeRoy M Drane
1815 Hemlock St.
Louisville, Ky.

Simmons Diary, l

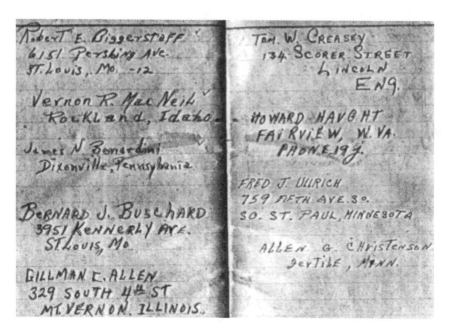

FRANCIS WAYNE PARSON
91 TRAFALGAR RD.
EGREMONT,
WALLASEY,
CHESHIRE,
ENG.

Clinton D. Bantz
416 N.S.BDWY,
WICHITA, Kan.

Adolph J. DiMinno
279 OAK ST.
New Britain Conn.

Charles R. Bistline
24 North Walnut St.
Hummelstawn, PA.

Oren E. Howard
417 N. 15th Street Sapulpa, OK
2316 Orange Ave.
Long Beach, California

George H. Dealtry.
43, Wortley Place,
Hemsworth.
Nr Pontefract.
Yorkshire. England.

Harold E. Shireman
1819 Conservative St.
New Albany, Indiana

Wilburn W. Seal
217 13th St.
Coleman, Texas

Simmons Diary, m

Robert E. Biggerstaff
6151 Pershing Ave.
St. Louis, Mo. -12.

Vernon R. MacNeil
Rockland, Idaho.

James N. Bonardini
Dixonville, Pennsylvania

Bernard J. Buschard
3951 Kennerly Ave.
St. Louis, Mo.

Gillman C. Allen
329 South 4th St
Mt. Vernon. Illinois.

Tom. W. Creasey
134 Scorer Street
Lincoln
ENG.

Howard Haught
Fairview, W. Va.
Phone 19 J.

Fred J. Ullrich
759 Fifth Ave. So.
So. St. Paul, Minnesota

Allen G. Christenson
Gertide, Minn.

Simmons Diary, n

SOCIETATEA CRUCEA ROȘIE A ROMANIEI
RED CROSS OF RUMANIA

received Sept 11th

GRATUITA
FREE OF CHARGE

CARTE POSTALA A PRIZONIERULUI DE RAZBOIU
PRISONERS OF WAR POST CARD

Destinatar: MR. LUTHER L. SIMMONS
Addressee
Adresa DELHI OKLAHOMA ROUTE 1
Address

Expeditor T/SGT. OVA W. SIMMONS
Sender
Adresa AMERICAN P.O.W. CAMP RUMANIA
Address

SOCIETATEA CRUCEA ROȘIE A ROMANIEI
RED CROSS OF RUMANIA

8 JUL. 1944
GRATUITA
FREE OF CHARGE

CARTE POSTALA A PRIZONIERULUI DE RAZBOIU
PRISONERS OF WAR POST CARD

Destinatar: MR. LUTHER L. SIMMONS
Addressee
Adresa DELHI OKLAHOMA
Address ROUTE - 1

Expeditor T/SGT. O.W. SIMMONS
Sender
Adresa AMERICAN PRISONER OF WAR IN RUMANIA
Address CAMP NO 13

Red Cross messages sent to Simmons's grandparents

POWs standing in crater made by German dive-bomber
(Sgt. Robert Bluhm, standing in center, with hand in pocket)

It's difficult, if not impossible, to imagine just what the American POWs felt as the days wore on at *"Hotel Bucharest"*—no freedom, lousy and insufficient food, no clean clothes, few beds, lice and bedbugs, no intermingling with family or old friends. It got old—in a hurry! Many harbored thoughts of trying to escape, but few took it any further than day dreaming or wishful thinking. One man, however, wasted no time in getting serious about it.

Sgt. Wilburn Seal grew up in the country where invention and innovation were a way of life—where, during the Great Depression, survival depended on ingenuity. His first day at Bucharest, he surveyed the situation, the lay-out of the prison—the old hospital near the railroad center on the northeast side of the city. He took note of the Rumanian guards who carried guns—they were loaded—and German guards who frequented the area. It didn't take long to develop a plan.

The POWs were permitted to walk around the grounds during the day, but they were not to cross the road or mingle with the curious citizens who ambled back and forth on their way to one place or another. Prisoners were assigned rooms, a dozen or so to each tiny cubicle furnished with two wooden beds having straw-filled mattresses. A dim, flickering light bulb dangled from a wire in the ceiling. No lumber, no wire, no hammer or nails, no tools—Sgt. Seal would have to make do with his hands.

Prisoners were confined to their rooms at nighttime although they were permitted access to hallways and toilets. Anyone wandering around outside after dark might be quickly dispatched—shot! The windows were equipped with iron bars set into solid concrete walls. Guards sat at the ends of the hallways, preventing anyone from leaving.

Having flown on multiple missions over Rumania, Sgt. Seal knew the lay of the land. He recalled the distance to neutral Yugoslavia as being almost two hundred miles to the west. The Adriatic Sea was another couple hundred miles beyond that. Escape to the west would be risky because of having to cross so much German-occupied territory. Less than a hundred miles to the east lay Russian-held territory, and his captors would likely not be expecting any *AWOL* prisoners there.

The escape plan was hatched and well underway within a few days of Sgt. Seal's capture. Every night after everyone had settled in, he occupied himself with cutting through one of the bars in the window opening. It would require two cuts—one at the top, the other at the bottom—in order to provide an opening through which he and any others could slither. Cutting through the heavy iron was going to be difficult, especially without a saw blade or other working tool.

Sgt. Seal worked on that bar for weeks, preparing it for removal. It had to be cut from behind in order to remain invisible from the front, for a guard would immediately notice any cuts across the front side. After many nights of tedious work, carefully rasping through the bar at the top and bottom, it was ready to be removed. Late one night after all was quiet, a couple of strong men twisted the bar from its mounting, leaving an opening barely large enough for a man's head to squeeze through. It was escape time—now or never!

How was a strong, muscular man going to get through such a narrow opening? The answer was quite simple: Following a three-month diet of limited watery soup and black bread, most of those men could slip past almost any opening through which a snake might slither!

One at a time—Seal and forty buddies wriggled through the opening and stealthily slipped off into the dark, undetected. They made haste, moving at night but laying low during the daytime, steadily moving toward the east. A week later, they reached the Danube River. At a Seal Family reunion a couple of years later, Seal related to his uncle, Quincy Ova Seal—father of Ova Wayne Simmons—that they considered trying to swim across, but it was impossible—the Danube was too wide and too deep (and, it was probably too fast and too cold!). After savoring their freedom for a time, they realized the futility of their situation. They probably allowed themselves to be captured by local peasants, for they were taken back to Bucharest in oxcarts. They wouldn't be there very long, however, because...

Things weren't going so well for the Germans. They certainly weren't going to give up the huge oil resources around Ploesti, but Bucharest was about to become a liability. King Michael (Mihai I) of Rumania announced on August 23rd that Rumania was capitulating to the Allies and would no longer be fighting for the Germans. Rumanian military personnel were ordered to take up arms against the Germans.

The Rumanian guards in charge of the American POWs simply opened the gates and allowed them to wander about the city. They had no place to go so they returned to the old hospital at nighttime where soup and hard bread were available.

Sgt. Seal and his crew mates were taken captive on May 18, 1944. His escape probably occurred sometime in early August, because he and the other escapees were free for only about two weeks.

Sgt. Wilburn Seal was awarded the Bronze Star for his work on the escape, along with numerous other medals for heroism and service. Fred Seal provided this account about his trip to Rumania and his father's escape from the Bucharest POW camp:

"With respect to our visit to the building in Romania where Dad was held captive, honestly, I don't remember that much. It was during the summer of 1969 which was twenty-five years after Dad was held captive there. It's now been over thirty-eight years since I was there. Dad's business had government contracts with the Air Force during the Vietnam 'conflict.' He conducted business with several USAF bases throughout Asia, notably Korea (Osan AFB), Philippines (Subic Bay), Thailand, and, of course, Vietnam (Bien Hoa). So, on summer break in 1969 (I was between sophomore and junior years at Texas Tech), Eliot (Fred's brother), and I went with Dad to call on these noted bases. So, our journey started east (USA) to west (Asia) and continued west on an around-the-world trek. It seemed like we hit about every major world city throughout southern Asia, the Middle East and many in Europe on the way home. Romania wasn't on our original itinerary. I believe we were in Singapore when Dad decided to incorporate Bucharest into our trip to show Eliot and me where he was held as a POW. He had found the site a few years prior while traveling with his second wife (Barbara Brown Seal). Barbara would have been able to shed much detail about how he rediscovered his POW site but, unfortunately, she is also now deceased. Anyway, I do remember that getting the visa for Romanian travel was quite difficult. As you know, it was during the peak of the cold war.

But Dad could be charming and persistent and he finally got us the required visas to travel there. What I remember about Bucharest is that it is a beautiful Old World city—lush parks, pleasant climate and elaborate, ornate buildings. The people seemed to be especially warm and friendly. They were most curious about America—and Americans—as they did not see many. My brother and I went to a disco and were approached by some very curious and friendly Russians. We consumed much vodka with them and departed the disco late at night as 'best friends.' This was within days of the USA's first successful moon landing. The Russians were relating to my brother and me as though it was us, rather than Neil Armstrong, that had taken the first lunar step. Getting back on point, we hired a Romanian guide that I remember to be particularly edgy. No doubt he thought he was—or he actually was—under state surveillance since he was in the company of Americans. With instructions and directions from Dad, we rode by taxi with the guide to the subject site that was referred to then as a 'military museum.' Sure enough, it was a museum that had old weapons, medieval armor, cannons and old Romanian medals on display. I am not sure, but I think I heard them say the building was previously a hospital or clinic but had been converted to a military museum after WW-II. I looked up museums in Bucharest on the Internet and found such a museum. The description of its contents fits exactly what I saw in 1969. However, the confusing part is the Internet says the museum was 'founded in 1972.' So, I do not know if the one I visited has been relocated, renovated or if the current listed military museum is even the same one. Anyway, the highlight of the trip was when Dad took us to one of the windows that had a missing iron bar. The museum had vertical iron 'security' bars. Dad stated that the missing iron bar was the very one he had sawed through in 1944 (I forgot what he said was his tool or how he obtained it for him and the other to escape). It was quite an astonishing moment. I have a mental picture to this day of that window and the missing bar."

The question remains: What tool did Sgt. Seal use to cut the iron bar from the window?

What would a country kid from Texas use? Quartz pebbles? Perhaps… Quartz gravel was all over the place! It would have been a simple matter to casually pick up a few sharp pebbles each day, wear them out at night and replace them the following day. Quartz, having a reference number of "7" on the *Mohs Scale* of hardness, is harder than iron and would therefore serve as a reasonable rasping tool.

GOODBYE, BUCHAREST! HELLO, ITALY!

Rumania was in a general state of confusion following the announcement of its capitulation to the Allied Forces on August 23, 1944. Rumanian petroleum was vital to the operation of the Nazi's war machines—most of Germany's military personnel in Rumania were concentrated near the oil refining complex around Ploesti. Bucharest didn't have the strategic importance as did Ploesti. Following the capitulation announcement and the fact that the Rumanian military forces no longer held allegiance to Germany, the German guards at the POW camps around Bucharest were left with few options. They would have much preferred to transport the POWs deep into German-held territory to be used as pawns in any future negotiations with the Allies, but this wasn't a practical option at the moment.

History has at times referred to the *'Liberation of Bucharest'* by the Soviets, but they didn't arrive at Bucharest until three days after the capitulation. They were undoubtedly disappointed at not being seen as the liberators of more than 1,100 Americans and other POWs. King Michael undoubtedly recognized that the Russians were on their way, but there were also other factors. At any rate, the American POWs were free—inside Rumania—with no immediate options for getting back to friendly territory. Two hundred miles of Nazi occupied territory lay between the POWs and freedom.

Ingenuity, a cornerstone of American achievement, quickly came into play. Countless obstacles would have to be overcome but, one by one, things began to happen. The first problem was that there was no way to pick up a thousand prisoners from one place and set them down six hundred miles away in another place—no operating rail system, no contiguous highways or roads, no waterways. Communication lines were in complete disarray throughout the region, making direct contact with the American military forces in Italy impossible. The Rumanian infrastructure was, by and large, destroyed. But, perhaps a miracle could be achieved. The highest ranking American POW, Col. James A. Gunn, was summoned to assess the situation. Col. Gunn arranged contact with the Rumanian government to learn whether someone might have a radio with which he could contact the 15th Air Force headquarters in Italy. Radio communication was achieved, but Col. Gunn wasn't able to provide the details of planning the mass escape of POWs—it was urgent that the enemy not intercept a message about an escape plan; otherwise, they'd take countermeasures. Col. Gunn was advised to fly to Bari, Italy, as quickly as possible.

At the moment, the Popesti Airdrome just outside the southeast edge of Bucharest was in the hands of the Rumanians. The German aviators had flown to other airfields from where they were launching repeated attacks on the American POW camps. Popesti was in bad shape, with numerous bomb craters, cracks and litter. On August 25, the major was provided an Italian aircraft with which to fly to Bari, but he'd barely gotten airborne when an engine conked out. He returned to the airport.

Col. Constantin Cantacuzino, a Rumanian fighter pilot ace who reportedly shot down dozens of enemy aircraft including American planes, offered Col. Gunn the use of a new Messerschmitt Me-109 fighter to fly to Bari—it wasn't an option, as Col. Gunn was a bomber pilot, not a fighter pilot. Cantacuzino then offered to fly Col. Gunn in the Me-109—but, that wasn't possible, either—or, was it? Cantacuzino removed four screws (or bolts?) from a side panel and pointed out how an individual might be squeezed into the confined radio compartment back of the pilot's seat. Col. Gunn agreed with the arrangement.

Col. Cantacuzino hastily painted an American flag on both sides of the small fighter plane and painted over the swastika markings on the wings. Maps were obtained and a route planned to the American airfield at San Giovani, Italy. On the afternoon of August 26th, Col. Gunn wriggled into the tiny space, and the panel was attached. Cantacuzino took off toward Italy flying high enough to avoid land-based antiaircraft gunfire, but he couldn't fly too high for fear of Col. Gunn freezing or dying from oxygen deprivation. The flight took two hours.

Captain Stanley L. DeGeer, flight operations officer for the 319th Fighter Squadron, 325th Fighter Group, was in the control tower when he received the report of a German Me-109 approaching the airport. Captain DeGeer ordered the gunners to hold their fire until the intent of the German plane could be determined. Otherwise, Gunn and Cantacuzino would have become past history. Major DeGeer stated that,

> *"When the Me-109 was first observed coming in, it was flying slow, with a nose-high attitude and its landing gear down. The pilot rolled the wings slowly to signal a friendly approach. When he landed and rolled to a stop, the MPs were all over the place. The pilot stepped out and told them that he had an American inside the plane, but nobody believed him. Someone produced a screwdriver and he removed a little panel. Sure enough, this bundle popped out and stood up! It was Col. James A. Gunn! Everyone was surprised, because we knew a Me-109 couldn't hold two men!*
>
> *"Well, I went over to see what was going on. This guy Cantacuzino spoke pretty good English. He asked about our P-51s—eighty shiny P-51s were lined up out there on the pads. He asked about taking a ride in one of them, so he was checked out and I gave him one to fly. We were the 'Checkertails,' you know. He flew that P-51 around for a while and brought it in for a perfect landing. He was good. He came over and told me, 'I like your P-51, but our Me-109s are a damn better plane.' He didn't understand how much better our '51s' were than his '109s,' because he hadn't been on the receiving end of a P-51."*

Col. Gunn was flown immediately to the 15th Air Force headquarters in Bari—a promontory jutting out into the Adriatic Sea. He described the situation to the superiors—over 1,100 American POWs stranded in Bucharest; no place to go; the Germans launching aerial attacks on the POW camp, day and night; prisoners running out of food and water; no medicines. Quick action was warranted. It was a risky endeavor, because the German bases from which the attacks were originating would first have to be neutralized.

Wing commanders were summoned and given the orders to proceed immediately with *'Project Gunn.'* Four P-51 aircraft, one piloted by Col. Cantacuzino, would proceed to Popesti airdrome in order to ensure that the area was solidly under the control of the Rumanians. Three of them would remain airborne while Cantacuzino landed to ascertain the status of the airport. He would then fire a special signal flare if all was safe. The three airborne P-51s would then climb high enough to communicate by radio, relaying a coded message to the 15th Air Force headquarters in Bari, through an intermediary aircraft flying over Yugoslavia. The messages would be in code language in order to keep the plan top secret. This part of the plan was achieved on the morning of August 29th.

Two specially fitted B-17 bombers with P-51 escort fighters departed Bari at noon and landed at Popesti Airdrome three hours later. With engines still running, they hastily discharged special personnel, equipment and Red Cross kits. The bombers wasted no time in getting airborne and headed back to Bari, because the escort planes were running on marginal fuel.

The special personnel went throughout Bucharest to locate and inform the POWs of the escape procedure. Transportation was arranged to move them from the old hospital prison and the other prison camps to Popesti Airdrome. Most of those interned at the old hospital camp had already left the area to avoid the constant aerial attacks from the Germans. Only forty or fifty seriously ill POWs remained at the hospital.

American bombers hit nearby German airfields in full force, knocking them completely out of action, thus paving the way for the evacuation to Bari. Weather conditions resulted in the breakdown of radio communications between Bucharest and Bari, so Cantacuzino was called upon again to fly a P-51 to Bari with a hand-delivered envelope carrying the message that all was ready at Popesti Airdrome.

Thirty-eight B-17 bombers from the 2nd and 97th Bomb Groups lifted off from Bari the morning of August 31, 1944, headed for Bucharest. One hundred-fifty P-51s (from the 31st, 325th, and 332nd Fighter Groups, including the 319th Squadron) and close to one hundred P-38s (from the 1st, 14th, and 82nd Fighter Groups) flew cover for the operation. The special teams had already scoured in and around Bucharest in order to inform all POWs of the plan to be transported back to Italy. As they arrived at the airport, they were arranged in groups of up to thirty men each, stationed every one hundred fifty feet along the taxi-way, with one man in charge of each group. It must have been an incredible sight for those POWs to see the first wave of twelve B-17s approach and land at around 10:30 AM. Each taxied up to a group of waiting airmen and quickly took them onboard. Two of the planes dropped off needed medical supplies and equipment, along with two doctors, one of whom was Col. W. R. "Randy" Lovelace, founder of Lovelace Hospital and Lovelace Healthcare System of New Mexico. These two men rushed to the old hospital to prepare the sick and bedfast for removal to the airport. A half-hour after landing, the planes took off for Bari! The second wave arrived shortly after 1:00 PM, took on the precious cargo and was off the ground within half an hour. Two of these bombers were equipped for transporting those needing urgent medical care along the way. By the end of the day's operation, more than seven hundred men had been evacuated to Bari!

The following day, September 2nd, another four hundred men were rounded up and evacuated. Several Rumanian people of means had taken in and were caring for some of the POWs. When they received word of the evacuation, the last twenty-nine prisoners were brought in and, on September 3rd, they were on their way home, along with the special personnel involved in the largest mass escape in history!

Sergeants Robert Bluhm and Wayne Simmons were the last two POWs to leave! They may have been hanging out with a Rumanian family and were late in receiving word of the mass escape, for they almost missed the last flight out of Bucharest! Simmons's diary—in the preceding chapter—recorded a number of addresses of fellow POWs, including the address of a Rumanian.

During this three-day period, 1,127 American POWs and thirty-four other prisoners, mostly British, were rescued and returned to their particular units. More than a hundred of them had been interned in Bucharest—apart from the others—since the fateful first mission to Ploesti on August 23, 1943, when almost a third of the bombers and crews was lost. Those who had parachuted to safety and were captured by the Germans spent more than a year as POWs. All the Bucharest prisoners were fortunate in not being marched around from camp to camp as the Germans retreated deeper into their own territory, for those POWs suffered the hardships of severe winters and torrid summers, sometimes having little if anything to eat for days at a time.

Upon landing at Bari, the Bucharest POWs were royally greeted. The first item of importance was delousing. The men shed the clothes they'd worn for months, were sprayed with insecticides to rid their bodies of lice and other ilk, showered and were issued new uniforms! They feasted on sandwiches and coffee and slept on comfortable cots that first night as *ex-prisoners of war!* And, they were paid! Over the next couple of days, they were returned to their original units where further jubilation took place.

For the crew of the *Shilay-Lee*, the war was over. For the crew of the *Hearts and Flowers*, the war was over. But, these men were still members of the United States Army Air Force until fulfilling their duties and being discharged. That would come a year later.

Surviving crew of the *Shilay-Lee*—now slim and trim—three days after returning to Italy; *Front row, L to R*: Altvater, Simmons, H. Moore; *Standing, L to R*: Christianson, MacNeil, Bluhm, Benardini, Barker (Note Simmons, wearing an Australian paratrooper cap and insignia, evidently traded while a POW.)

The former POWs were provided with comfortable quarters and every conceivable luxury within reason—food, drinks, candy, cigarettes—while waiting. It wasn't long.

On September 10 and 11, 1944, the men from the *Hearts and Flowers* and the *Shilay-Lee*, along with several hundred other ex-prisoners, were transported in trucks to Naples. They boarded the Greek steamer, *Athos-II*, and sailed to the Straits of Gibraltar on September 13th. The remainder of the trip wasn't without incident—a boiler failed, the ship encountered the tail end of a hurricane, and there were a couple of rough days at sea. The ship arrived in New York Harbor on September 26th, following a fourteen-day voyage.

The *boys-turned-men*—ex-prisoners of the Nazis—were given promotions and well-deserved thirty-day furloughs home. Following high quality time with family and friends, the airmen boarded trains all across the country and headed to Miami Beach for a couple of weeks of R & R. From there, they went to St. Petersburg for two weeks, then back to Miami Beach. Most of the men requested assignments back near their homes. T/Sgt. Bluhm took the train to Chanute Field near Rantoul, Illinois, where he spent the next eight months as an instructor at a welding school. T/Sergeants Wilburn Seal and Raymond Crouch returned to west Texas and served as instructors at Reese AFB for the next eight months. T/Sgt. Wayne Simmons was assigned to Will Rogers AFB where he applied his skills in radio and electronics. Lt. Leo Bollei was sent to Douglas, Arizona, to fly B-25 twin-engine bombers and was later given an assignment back near Detroit, Michigan. This was pretty much the pattern for the other former prisoners at Bucharest.

On August 23, 1945, T/Sgt. Robert Bluhm went by train to Fort Sheridan near Chicago for a week of processing and was discharged on August 30. T/Sgt. Wayne Simmons was discharged at Fort Sheridan, as were most of the men of the *Hearts and Flowers* and the *Shilay-Lee*.

Back in Coleman, Texas, Sgt. Wilburn W. Seal was interviewed by a hometown news reporter. A copy of the news clipping follows on the next page.

Wilburn Seal Wouldn't Have Given Nickel For His Life While He Was Prisoner; He's Visiting in City

"I didn't think I would ever be home again and I wouldn't have given a nickel for my life."

That's the way T/Sgt. Wilburn W. (Pee Wee) Seal, 20, son of Mr. and Mrs. B. Seal, 217 13th Street, felt while being held a prisoner of war from May 18 until August 31 of this year.

"We were bombed by the English, Russians, Americans and Germans during the time we were being held in a hospital, just three blocks from the target, in Bucharest," Sgt. Seal declared.

The handsome young engineer was shot down over Ploesti on his 22nd mission over Europe and the seventh over the important Romanian oil center. Two of the engines on his B-17 Flying Fortress had been knocked out by German flak and a third had been set afire by German fighters.

At 20,000 feet Sgt. Seal and his companions bailed out and landed at Alexandra, which is near Ploesti. The 36 bombers in his formation had been "jumped" by 200 German fighters. Incidentally, the Coleman soldier shot down three German fighters and got two probables while his ship was credited with knocking down seven German ships and getting eight more probables.

Wilburn's crew was lucky, for no serious injuries were received, but it was one of the few crews that was so fortunate.

On reaching the ground the airmen were taken into custody by the Romanians who soon carried them to a military garrison at Bucharest. A short time later they were carried to a hospital, where he learned the receiving end of the bombing game. The American, English and Russian airmen were trying to hit a certain target only three blocks away while the Germans dive bombed the hospital area because they knew Americans were being held there. Wilburn states he was blown out of a window on two occasions by the bomb concussions.

Food Is Poor

The Romanians treated the prisoners kindly but were unable to furnish better food than soup and sour bread. The beds were so infested with lice that Sgt. Seal and many other boys slept on the floor.

Fortunately, he was there when the weather was not too hot or too cold and he had his full uniform on when he jumped. Other prisoners of war weren't so lucky, however, as at least half of them did not have shoes.

When the Romanian government capitulated to Russia the Allied prisoners of war were released and Sgt. Seal flew from Bucharest to Bari, Italy, on Aug. 31. Since that time he has been anxiously awaiting the time when he could get back home.

Now that he is back, he can't make up his mind as to whether he wants to go to Officers Candidate School, become a flying cadet, accept a permanent station in the U. S., or accept that promotion to master sergeant that was promised to him in Italy. He likes flying and fighting and likely he will choose the course that will get him back in action the quickest.

He holds the Air Medal and five clusters, the Purple Heart, the Distinguished Flying Cross, given for the raid over Ploesti when his plane was shot down, the Purple Heart, given for the injury received during the same Ploesti raid, and the Bronze Star, given for his work on the "escape committee" while he was a POW. He aided 40 American boys to escape from the prison camp during the last week he was there.

Sgt. Seal is a native of Coleman, born on Dec. 21, 1923, and a graduate of the local high school (1942) For a while he operated the Cities Service Agency here, but joined the AAF on Nov. 1, 1942. He received training at Amarillo, the Boeing factory, and at Las Vegas gunnery school.

He went to Italy, via South America and North Africa, on Feb. 23, 1944.

MAJOR STANLEY L. DEGEER, P-51 PILOT

Stanley L. DeGeer, longtime friend and associate of the author, was a fighter pilot with the 15th Air Force based in Italy. He arrived at Celone Airfield around the time of the Normandy Invasion and was assigned to the 15th Air Force, 325th Fighter Group, 319th Squadron. Stan was older than most other pilots, having been born in 1916 and arriving in the combat zone at the age of twenty-eight. He enlisted in the Army Air Corps prior to the attack on Pearl Harbor, passed the physical and mental tests and was accepted in the Aviation Cadet program. Stan's humor was never far away!

> *"When I was given a physical exam, doctors sat on either side and looked into my ears. They couldn't see each other, so I was deemed physically fit."*

According to Stan, he barely passed the tests, barely escaped washing out as a pilot trainee, and was near the last on every list of accomplishments. It's highly probable that he was barely telling the truth—a most modest gentleman.

Two-thirds of his Primary Flight Training class 'washed out' and, according to Stan, he could have been the next one on the list. But, he wasn't. He'd mastered the 'wood-and-fabric' Fairchild PT-19 at Tulsa

Municipal Airport, the BT-13 'Vultee Vibrator' at Enid Army Airfield (OK) and was looking forward to moving up to the A-20 twin-engine light bomber.

Stan describes his military training:

"After I completed Basic Flight Training, I applied for— and thought I was given the choice of going to—twin-engine for my Advanced Flight Training. However, when I got my orders, the Air Corps suggested that I might like to go to Foster Field, Texas, for training in the single-engine AT-6—in Navy lingo, the SJN. I quickly decided that was exactly what I wanted to do! The right way? The wrong way? No! The Army way!

"Now, the AT-6 was, and is, a SUPER airplane. Many are still flying. It has a retractable landing gear, hydraulic flaps, controllable pitch prop—all the good stuff the PT-19 and BT-13 lacked. I soon felt fairly comfortable in it,

"There were three or four especially dangerous, stressful times for me in pilot training—the first solo, the first solo cross-country, learning night flying on a crowded field, and night cross-countries. Identifying landmarks over the unfamiliar, vast, Texas plains (night or day) was quite a challenge. I got lost more than once before I learned to carefully read those instruments and maps.

"With the attack on Pearl Harbor, everything went on a War Emergency basis! We were rushed through a two-year program in about seven months. They had taken me as a grungy civilian and produced a pilot, officer, and gentleman (by act of Congress). I had two hundred hours in the air and, with a little training in a combat airplane, would be ready to take on the enemy. Anyway, that was the theory.

"We must remember—rushed training went on for the tank corps, artillery, mechanized cavalry, soldiers, sailors, and marines—by the millions—all over the country. Ordinary people, volunteers and draftees became GIs and were quickly transformed into formidable fighting forces. Formidable? Well, maybe!

"During later stages of my training, and with no idea what my assignment might be, Eloise (my bride to be!) had traveled to Texas, accompanied by her mother—her father would have none of it—and, on July 21, 1942, we were married.

"Upon graduation, would I be ready for combat? In retrospect, I feel I would have proved easy prey for an experienced enemy pilot. The two hundred hours of training just got me into the air. Now, I know effective combat pilots have self-discipline, organization, flying ability, courage, and luck. At the time, about all I had going for me was the luck.

"September 6, 1942, the day of becoming an Office & Gentleman, when I put on those 2nd Lieutenant bars and that officers cap, I moved immediately into a different world. I was no longer 'Mister.' I was 'Lieutenant,' or 'Sir.' And, enlisted men saluted me!

"The next morning, I went to the operations office to get my combat assignment. Wonder of wonders! Out of a class of maybe two hundred, I was one of a half-dozen chosen to stay at Foster Field as an Advanced Flight Instructor!"

Stan related how he learned much while teaching those first two or three classes of Aviation Cadets—mostly the things he hadn't learned well during his own flight training. He recalled how he'd developed into a reasonably confident pilot during those years. He moved up to Flight Leader in the Gulf Coast Training Command, on to Commanding Officer of a training squadron, and promoted to First Lieutenant.

As experienced pilots completed combat tours, returned and were assigned as flight instructors, Lt. DeGeer found himself in the uncomfortable position of being in command of *Captains* and an occasional *Major*. So, he applied for a combat assignment. The Group Operations Officer recommended Stan for a soft assignment flying patrol missions out of Panama, but he declined.

Lt. DeGeer left his wife with her folks in Colorado Springs and continued on to Millville, New Jersey, to train in the P-47 Thunderbolt—the most massive, powerful fighter plane in the world. It boasted two thousand horsepower and was equipped with eight 50-calibre machine guns. A couple of months and many experiences later, Lt. DeGeer was sent to the embarkation port at Newport News, Virginia, where he boarded an LST—Tank Landing Ship—in a convoy of seventy-two ships headed for the Mediterranean. German U-boats were a constant menace but, in early June of 1944, he arrived safely in Italy where he was assigned to the 319ᵗʰ Fighter Squadron of the 325ᵗʰ Fighter Group. To his amazement and utter joy, he learned that he'd be flying a new 'secret' fighter plane—the super secret, long range, high altitude, P-51 Mustang!

It was an exciting moment when they were taken to the flight line where all those beautiful, shiny new P-51s were lined up. As for being checked out in them—they were told, "If you can fly a P-47, you'll have no trouble with the P-51!" They were right.

Upon reporting for duty, Lt. DeGeer was shocked to learn that he'd been appointed Assistant Operations Officer for the *319ᵗʰ*. This was unusual, because operations officers were usually Captains and Majors. The situation was that the *319ᵗʰ* had lost half its planes and pilots during recent missions (before the P-51s arrived), and the Chief Operations Officer, a Lt. Colonel and West Point graduate, had been 'busted' to a Captain after getting crossed up with General Nathan Twining, the Commanding General of the 15ᵗʰ Air Force. The demoted officer was headed out, so Stan was made the Operations Officer. As such, he was responsible for planning the missions for the pilots and fighter planes of the *319ᵗʰ*. As Stan put it, *"I thought they must be joking!"*

> *"How did I manage it all? First, I got the TO (Tables of Organization), then reassigned flying personnel into flights directed by Flight Leaders. Did I have help? You bet! Four knowledgeable, efficient, patient Sergeants guided me and did the daily office work.*
>
> *"The 325's main missions were high altitude escort for long range bombers—the B-17s and B-24s. We flew deep into enemy territory. We also flew an occasional strafing mission or fighter sweep, just to keep the old adrenaline pumping, and boy did that do it! An exploding locomotive or ammunition car put a lot of debris into the air!*
>
> *"As it turned out, my first mission was a milk run; we all flew out, the bombers bombed, and we flew back.*

And being in a fighter appeared relative safe, because we flew around the flak clouds put up by the German 88mm antiaircraft guns. The bombers had to fly through it, and some didn't make it.

"Our second mission changed my mind. We escorted bombers over the target near Budapest, Hungary. We approached at almost thirty thousand feet, but flying even higher were planes drawing contrails as they flew a crisscross pattern. I thought, 'Those just might be enemy fighters.' They were! Those Me109s soon attacked our bombers as we went after them.

"My flight leader, with me as cover, shot one down. Another, after a run at the bombers, zipped under us and into the safety of a cloud before either of us could get him. My Catholic tent mate asked if I prayed before a mission. I said, 'No. If the German I tangle with has prayed, that might frustrate God!'

"I flew five missions in eight days during which we had eight dog fights—on the job training! When I asked my tent mate if these were his ideas of 'milk runs,' he said 'It won't last.'

"I found the P-51 was a truly superior plane and soon felt comfortable in it. The empty ache in my stomach preceding a mission eased, once I strapped the plane on and fired up that powerful Merlin engine. It gave us power to reach thirty-three thousand feet.

"Guys came and went. Some got shot down, but many completed their missions and returned to the States. However, support personnel were there for the duration. For most, that meant three years over there.

"As Operations Officer, I had some flexibility. For one thing, I got to—or had to—put my own name on the list when I wanted to fly a mission. I often wondered, on any given day, if I had signed my own death warrant. My main duties, however, were to train the flight leaders and replacement pilots, and to oversee the missions."

Stan flew missions all over Europe, generally within a radius of up to six hundred miles of his base near Celone, Italy. The missions mostly involved flying escort for B-17 and B-24 bombers, but they also included strafing missions to knock out locomotives and other targets of opportunity, or enemy harassment. He described one interesting mission in particular:

"On the mission, we were flying escort for a large group of B-24 heavy bombers headed toward a high priority target in Germany. We'd departed our base near Celone a few hours earlier. The bombers were flying at elevations ranging around twenty thousand feet, and my P-51 fighter squadron was following at around thirty thousand feet. Towering cumulus clouds floated under and around us, with occasional breaks through which we could see the landscape below.

"All of a sudden, off to my left, I caught a brief glimpse of three German Me-210 twin-engine fighter planes a couple of thousand feet below, darting under the clouds in a tight "V" formation. Within seconds, they'd passed beneath us and momentarily reappeared off to the right using the clouds for cover. Estimating where they would probably emerge from the next cloud, I rolled to the right in inverted position and descended for the attack.

"Suddenly, they emerged from cloud cover as they banked to the left, heading toward the bombers. At that instant, the lead pilot happened to glance up and see me coming straight down at them. Realizing 'he was dead,' gut instinct evidently caused him to jerk his plane sharply to the right—wrong move! The other Me-210s, unable to react swiftly enough, chewed directly into the tail of the lead plane, destroying all three in the blink of an eye. The resulting crash reduced the German planes to metal parts and pieces as the debris dispersed into the clouds below.

"A few seconds later, a German pilot suddenly dropped from the cloud—directly in front of me—with his parachute unfurling. The force from the rapid deceleration literally jerked off his black knee-high boots. There he was, right in my sights, an easy target! One burst from my 50-mm guns would end his war, but...

"No! I couldn't shoot an unarmed enemy warrior! I quickly rolled to the left, missing him by inches, and zipped past at 250 mph—so close I could see the expression on his face as he appeared to snap to attention! I don't know who was more frightened, him or me. I climbed to rejoin my buddies and carry on the fight.

"I've often wondered what it was like for that guy to walk out of those mountains barefooted. I also wonder what kind of story he told his family after the war, or if he even lived to tell it."

[Note: Stan remarked that the German fighter pilots never seemed to have figured out that, when flying at high altitude, they should keep their boots zipped to the top, even if their feet got overly warm. It was a common occurrence when an enemy pilot lost one or both boots at the moment his chute jerked sharply. Stan remarked that this particular pilot may have snapped to attention as he whizzed by, but Stan was too preoccupied with missing him while at the same time trying to avoid debris from the three-plane pile-up. In researching the active German fighter aircraft during the early summer of 1944, most Me-210s were out of service, and many Me-310s were being replaced by the latest version—the Me-410. All three versions appeared nearly identical, so it is the author's belief that these particular planes were more likely to have been Me-310s or Me-410s.]

When asked what kind of footwear he wore on missions, Stan replied,

"I always wore those old fashioned G.I. boots—the lace-up kind. If I'm gonna get shot down somewhere over those Alps, I sure don't want to have any problems hiking out!"

DeGeer had more than his share of exciting and last-second decisions to make. Following the three-plane pile up of the Messerschmitt fighter planes, he climbed back up to join his buddies flying escort for the B-24s. But, as he searched the sky for them, he spotted a lone Me-210:

> *"I poured on the coals to my P-51 and quickly moved in on his tail. Evidently, no one on the 210 saw me coming, because he took no evasive action, and his tail gunner didn't fire at me. In fact, it was so easy that I felt uneasy. I rolled out a little to double-check, and there was a big Red Star on the side of a Russian plane, which looked like the 210. 'Thank you, Lord!' Had I gone back to base with film in my gun camera of me shooting down a Russian—our ally—I would have been in big trouble!*
>
> *"As I turned to head back to Italy, in the distance I saw what appeared to be a single engine Me-109. So, I went after him. As I closed, he looked like a new model British Spitfire. What a dilemma! Was it a captured 'Spit' flown by a German? Or, what was a British plane doing down here in 'our' war? It didn't matter though, because the pilot saw me coming, went to full power and headed west. By this time, I was deep in enemy territory and decided it would be wise to head back to base some four hundred miles south, and come back another day."*

Lt. DeGeer flew scores of missions as a pilot and Operations Officer for the *319th*—carrying out the duties of a Major while still a Lieutenant. On August 23, 1944, he was promoted to Captain, just as the King of Rumania was preparing to announce the capitulation of Rumania to the Allied Forces. One of DeGeer's first jobs as 'Captain DeGeer' was organizing his P-51 squadron to coordinate with the mass evacuation of 1,127 American POWs from Bucharest to Italy. His involvement and interaction with the Rumanian pilot, Col. Constantin Cantacuzino, is described in Chapter 12.

DeGeer's missions as Operations Officer, pilot and member of the famous "Checkertail Clan" continued through the summer of 1944 and up into the late spring of 1945. He recalled flying on raids to Ploesti, Rumania, five days in a row, and on raids to Berlin, Vienna, and other sites of strategic importance to the Nazis. The continual bombardment and attacks eventually wore down the enemy to the point that aerial resistance was on the verge of collapse.

Many months and missions after DeGeer arrived in the combat theater of Europe, his flying days came to an abrupt halt. He was lucky for not having been shot down while, at the same time, he'd dealt out more than his fair share of destruction on the enemy. His Commanding Officer—the individual on whom DeGeer depended for promotion—was killed in a plane crash. Here was Captain DeGeer who'd filled the position of Operations Officer for nearly a year—a position that required the rank of Major—who, now, may never get that promotion.

A few days later, Captain DeGeer and three other pilots were headed to the Officers Club when they were sideswiped by a weapons carrier—a vehicle about three times as large as their jeep.

"It flipped us off the road, but I was the only one seriously injured in either vehicle. The side-mounted spare tire of the Weapons Carrier hit my left arm and nearly tore it off. I had fifteen fractures, from the tips of my fingers up into my jaw, and the head of the humerus was shattered. My hand was split open, and the radius and ulna were snapped and sticking out the back of my arm. To make matters worse, we landed in thorny bushes. In my battered condition, my survival seemed unlikely. Loss of blood alone should have killed me. I was getting thorns out for months.

"I was on the ground only a minute or two when a Flight Surgeon from one of the other squadrons came by. They loaded us into the ambulance and rushed us to a nearby hospital. They stemmed the bleeding, immobilized my mangled arm, sedated me, pumped plenty of the new drug, penicillin, into me, and put me to bed. No operation was performed at that time. They wanted to see whether I'd live.

"After eleven days, I gained enough strength for them to operate. They performed an open reduction on the radius—the metal plate is still in my arm—and reattached my crazy bone; the screw is still there. A full cast was put on my arm. Two of the doctors had wanted to amputate, but the old colonel in charge said, 'Oh, we can always take it off. Let's see if we can put it together.'"

HOME IS WHERE THE HEART IS

Over the space of three weeks, life for each of these aviators had taken a dramatic turn. The contrast could hardly have been greater—from malnourished, maltreated subjects of the Nazis to the good life back in the United States of America! Free, at last! During their captivity, they could only dream of wives or girlfriends, steak and eggs, or a stroll in the park. Now, it had all changed.

How did these guys spend their time after arriving back on American soil? Well, first, there were a bunch of required forms to be filled out, after which they had tracks to make!

Julius Altvater headed down to Packanack Lake, New Jersey, to visit his sister, Mrs. Anna Clinch, while Robert Barker left immediately to go see his girlfriend, Rae, at Lincoln, Nebraska. Hugh Moore alternated between his mother's home in Philadelphia and New York City. Vernon MacNeil traveled to Rockland, Idaho, to spend time with his parents, Mr. and Mrs. Murvel MacNeil, and family. Robert Bluhm went to see his mother, Mrs. Anna Bluhm, his lovely girlfriend, Larene, and others around the village of Clayton, Illinois.

James Benardini stopped by to visit his mother in Dixonville, Pennsylvania, before continuing to Georgia to see his girlfriend, Dorothy. Allen Christianson traveled to his mother's home in Fertile, Minnesota while Douglas Millar, the photographer, went to visit his mother and step-father down in Bluefield, West Virginia. Wayne Simmons boarded the train and headed for his home in rural, southwest Oklahoma to see a host of relatives, friends and, his pretty girlfriend, Verna Lou.

Wilburn Seal could hardly wait to get back to Coleman, Texas to greet his parents, Burbridge and Ollie Seal, who were greatly relieved that he'd gotten home safely—and, of course, his beautiful girlfriend, Joyce. Edward Buffington rode the train to Anderson, Texas, where his parents, Mr. and Mrs. Thomas Buffington, and other family anxiously awaited his arrival.

For Sydney Fisher, it was just an hour to his parents' home in Albany but, for Raymond Crouch, it was a long ride on the rails to Amarillo, Texas, to meet up with his wife, Thelma. Leo Bollei's mother, Madelane, was happy to see her son once again in Detroit.

William Karlovitz was thrilled to be back in Chicago to visit his mother and family, as was Keith Winder, back in Cleveland. His father, Clarence, and mother were delighted he'd made it back. Jack Haney returned to his home near Yakima, Washington and spent time with his brother, Douglas, and other family. Joseph Cutrone hung out at his home in New York City; his father, James, and the rest of the family were overjoyed to see him. Mr. and Mrs. Fritz Jensen were greatly relieved that their son, Leslie Jensen, was back in Los Angeles.

The leaves were well deserved and greatly appreciated by these former prisoners of war. For each, there was some measure of excitement. As for Wayne Simmons, he could hardly contain himself. He'd left his beautiful girlfriend back in high school, and they had plans. Upon arriving back in the rural community of Delhi, Oklahoma, on October 5, 1944, as described by Verna Lou sixty-six years later,

> *"We were at Roy and Selene Simmons's house when Roy said, 'If you two are going to get married, why not get married tomorrow?' So, we did! We'd been engaged a year."*

Wayne's uncle, Roy Simmons, drove them into Sayre and on October 6th, the day following his return from the war, Wayne—age twenty—and Verna Louise Eastham—age seventeen— processed a marriage license at the Beckham County Courthouse and were married in a quiet ceremony at a local church shortly afterward. Wayne's Uncle

Roy swore that both were of legal age (Wayne, 21, and Verna, 18), thus facilitating their marriage.

Robert Bluhm, now twenty-four years of age, wasted no time after returning home on October 5, 1944. He and his lovely girlfriend, Larene Flesner, were married at Golden, Illinois, on October 8th.

James N. Benardini—age twenty-three—and Dorothy E. Lawson—age nineteen—were married in Walker County, Georgia, on October 13.

Robert J. Barker, now twenty-five, and his girlfriend, Rae, from Lincoln, Nebraska, married and set up housekeeping in New York.

Their leaves ended all too soon, but they would eventually transition back into civilian life. For a few, the military would be their lives for the next several years but, for most, they were ready to get back to whatever kind of 'normal' lives they could recover. James Benardini, Robert Barker and Wayne Simmons were anxious to start 'new' lives with their brides while Raymond Crouch was anxious to pick up where he'd left off with his wife, Thelma. Leo Bollei, Wilburn Seal, and Julius Altvater elected to stay in the military, at least for the time being, Altvater made a career in the Air Force and achieved the rank of major before retiring in 1964.

Vernon MacNeil returned to agricultural activities in his native Idaho where he was also an active outdoorsman and sportsman. Wayne Simmons utilized his electronics training and skills from the Air Force to land a position in the electronics industry with the General Electric Company in Tulsa, Oklahoma.

Leslie Jensen returned to Los Angeles and took up enforcement work with the Los Angeles Police Department, a position he held for many years, up until the time his old crew buddies lost track of him. Jack Haney returned to his home state of Washington and appears to be living near Yakima at this time. Attempts to communicate with him weren't successful.

Joseph Cutrone kept contact with his crew buddies for many years from his home in New York City. Raymond Crouch reported having communicated with Cutrone as late as 1975. Keith Winder was last heard from in Cleveland. William Karlovitz, living in Illinois, and Leo Bollei, living north of Detroit, maintained frequent contact and, according to Bollei, often visited at each other's homes up until around 2005.

Leo Bollei was transferred to Douglas, Arizona, following his leave and placed in flight training on the Mitchell B-25 light bomber. He was sent to the flight training school at San Antonio, Texas, and later returned to Douglas. He then requested an assignment near Detroit in order to be closer to home. He married not long afterward and, after assignments in France and England, retired in Michigan where he and his son, Rick, reside. Over the years, he remained in contact with his former crew and stopped to visit with them whenever traveling around the country. Bollei's wife, Elizabeth, passed away in 2008.

Joe Cutrone returned to White Plains, New York but remained in close contact with his old crew mates. Joe was active in the *Association of the Former Prisoners of War in Rumania.*

Raymond Crouch returned home to pick up where he'd left off. He and his wife, Thelma, raised three children, one of whom is Woody Crouch, major contributor to this work. Raymond was very active in Veterans affairs throughout his life. Wilburn Seal accepted a transfer to Amarillo Air Force Base in Texas after returning from Italy. He also worked on special assignments at Walker Air Force Base in NM and at Reese Air Force Base in Texas. He achieved the rank of lieutenant before being discharged. He was recalled to active duty for several years during the Korean War. Returning to Lubbock, Texas, he returned to civilian life but remained active in technological enterprises, owning and flying his own aircraft in civil applications. He and his wife, Joyce, had four children—Jeanette, Fred, Eliot and David. Fred and Jeanette were major contributors to, and great motivation for, this work.

Little else is known about the professional lives of the others except for Stanley DeGeer.

After recuperating sufficiently to be transported, Captain DeGeer was flown home from Italy as a litter patient and treated at three different hospitals over the course of the next several months. He underwent two more surgeries at William Beaumont Army Medical Center at El Paso, Texas. The war ended, and he was ordered to meet with the retirement board. Much to his surprise, he was informed that he had a lot of time in grade—he was promoted to Major! Major Stanley L. DeGeer finally got to return home!

LOOKING BACK OVER TIME

TWENTY-FOUR INCREDIBLE AIRMEN

More than six decades have passed since these twenty-four of America's finest—men of *The Greatest Generation*—served their country in the war to end all wars. Having been born early in the twentieth century, only a few remain today. It would be so easy to simply ignore them, to forget about the sacrifices they and their families made to protect and preserve the United States of America. This isn't going to happen!

These twenty-four airmen played a vital role in dismantling the Nazi war machine by shutting off its life blood—petroleum. They and fellow soldiers—from Europe to the Pacific—paid dearly in order to bring down the evil empires of Nazi Germany and Imperial Japan.

The bombing campaigns against the Germans also focused on aircraft production plants, railroad marshalling yards, submarine pens, sea ports, ball bearing factories, industrial centers, infrastructure and other petroleum facilities. The oil refining complex near Ploesti, Rumania—at the top of the list in strategic importance to the Germans—was an especially hazardous and well defended target.

The first bombing mission to Ploesti—August 23rd, 1943—was from faraway Africa. Tragically, a third of the aircraft and crews were lost. The next mission to Ploesti wasn't carried out until early spring of 1944, after the Americans had established bases in Italy. The raids on Ploesti began on April 5, 1944, and increased in frequency and intensity throughout the spring and summer. By the time the *Shilay-Lee* and *Hearts and Flowers* were blown out of the skies in May of 1944, the Nazis had their backs to the wall—they could not manage damage control due to the continuous onslaught of the American bombers returning to rain death and destruction almost every day. There came the time when the bad guys had to give up their oil resources at Ploesti and retreat back into *the Fatherland*. Having lost more than half their petroleum supplies by early summer of 1944, it was only a matter of time until the Nazi war machinery ground to a halt.

The destruction of the Concordia Vega Oil Refinery northwest of Ploesti, Rumania, is evident in this photograph:

Concordia Vega Oil Refinery; Ploesti, Rumania, September, 1944

As of July 1, 2010, the following information is known about the individuals featured in this book:

Ova Wayne Simmons, born March 7, 1924, passed away of brain tumor in Oklahoma on September 6, 1956, at only thirty-two years of age, leaving his wife, Verna Lou Eastham Simmons, and three young children—Robert Wayne, Roy Vaughn (a Vietnam Navy Veteran who passed away in 2003), and Linda. Wayne's head injury from enemy antiaircraft fire never completely healed and may have hastened his death.

Francis M. Boyle, born in 1918, died when the plane he was piloting, the *Shilay-Lee,* exploded and crashed in western Rumania on May 5, 1944. He was only twenty-six. He was survived by his wife, Betty Brooks Boyle, in Lansing, Michigan.

Leo Bollei was born in Michigan in 1921. He is eighty-nine years of age, doing well, and resides in Sterling Heights, Michigan.

Robert M. Bluhm, born June 30, 1920, in Herkimer, Kansas, passed away on March 27, 2008, in Clayton, Illinois. He was nearing eighty-eight. His wife, Larine Flesner Bluhm, passed away in 1994. Their son and daughter, Gene Bluhm and Phyllis Bluhm Erber, live nearby.

John Donner, born December 18, 1918, in Pennsylvania, passed away in Midland, Minnesota in September, 1984, at the age of sixty-six.

Edward Buffington, born July 20, 1918, at Anderson, Texas, passed away January 10, 2003, in Grimes County, Texas. Edward was eighty-four years of age.

Vernon MacNeil, born March 27, 1923, passed away in Idaho on December 1, 2009, at the age of eighty-seven. His wife, Maureen Riddle MacNeil preceded him three months earlier.

Julius A. Altvater, born July 26, 1920, passed away on June 10, 2003, at the age of eighty-three. He lived at Bragg, California.

James N. Benardini, born in 1921, lives near Jacksonville, Florida, with his wife, Dorothy Lawson Benardini. One of their sons, or grandsons, appears to be a world renowned microbiologist.

Sidney Fisher was born February 19, 1926, in Massachusetts. He passed away in Jacksonville, Florida, on July 29, 2006, at the age of eighty.

Raymond Crouch was born on June 13, 1917, in Illinois and passed away on May 11, 1994, in Amarillo, Texas, at the age of seventy-seven.

Keith Winder was born in Ohio on September 22, 1916. He passed away on July 22, 1994, in Riverside County, California at the age of seventy-eight.

Hugh M. Moore, born June 27, 1917, passed away on October 4, 2003, in Philadelphia, at the age of eighty-six.

Robert J. Barker, born June 4, 1919, passed away in December, 1977, in Lucerne County, Pennsylvania, at the age of fifty-eight.

Allen G. Christianson was born in 1920, in Fertile, Minnesota. His NARA enlistment records are missing. Allen, now 90, and Norma Christianson, age 87, appear to be living in Portland, Oregon.

Frederick "Sam" Moore, born in 1918, in Virginia, was killed when an enemy shell exploded behind him as he co-piloted the *Shilay-Lee* over Ploesti, Rumania, on May 5, 1944. Sam was only twenty-six. He was survived by his wife, Iris.

William Karlovitz, born November 21, 1917, in Cook County, Illinois, passed away in Mount Prospect, Illinois, on August 6, 2006. He was nearing eighty-nine years of age.

Jack R. Haney, born near Yakima, Washington, in 1920, would be 90 years of age and may be living in Yakima.

Douglas Millar was born June 6, 1923, near Bluefield, West Virginia and passed away at Winston-Salem, North Carolina, on December 12, 2000, at the age of seventy-seven.

Robert Jackson was born in Texas around 1920. He was reported lost in a plane crash in the Adriatic Sea in 1944. He would have been only about 24 years of age.

Joseph J. Cutrone was born in New York on April 13, 1917, and passed away on July 2, 2005, in Queens, New York. He was eighty-eight years of age.

Wilburn W. Seal was born near Coleman, Texas on December 21, 1923. He lost his life in a tragic automobile accident near McAllen, Texas, on August 24, 1974, at the age of fifty.

Leslie M. Jensen, born October 25, 1919, in California, passed away in July of 1974, in Santa Clara, California. He was nearing fifty-five years of age.

Stanley L. DeGeer was born in Colorado on August 15, 1916, and passed away in Albuquerque, New Mexico, on December 1, 2009. He was in his 94th year.

What kind of *"Thank You"* did these *True American Heroes* receive? A grateful America mourned the loss of those who sacrificed their lives and welcomed those who returned. This era could rightfully be described as the highest point in American History—an era when all Americans marched to the same drumbeat.

These men were honored by the president of the United States, and by the military—with ribbons, medals, and citations—for their service, bravery, and accomplishment. Although each was highly decorated, his decorations and medals were exhibited only on rare occasions. Both the *Hearts and Flowers* and the *Shilay-Lee* received Distinguished Unit Citations—awarded for successful completion of extremely hazardous missions while under continuous, severe enemy resistance. Each airman was awarded four or more high-level medals reserved for greatest accomplishment while under extreme combat duress, in addition to numerous ribbons for good conduct, combat service in Africa and Italy, internment as a prisoner of war, and other involvement. Each received medals for meritorious service beyond the regular sphere of ordinary military service. These included the Air Medal for achievement during extremely hazardous combat duty and Oak Leaf Clusters for involvement in especially dangerous aerial warfare. Several were awarded the Purple Heart for combat related injuries, including:

- T/Sgt Wayne Simmons, combat injury—burns and head injury from enemy anti-aircraft shrapnel
- Lt. Francis Boyle, killed in action—went down with the *Shilay-Lee*

- T/Sgt Robert Bluhm, combat injury—head injury from enemy anti-aircraft shrapnel
- Lt. Julius Altvater, combat injury—burns to hands and face from fire and explosion on the *Shilay-Lee*
- T/Sgt. James Benardini, combat injury—burns to hands and face from fire and explosion on the *Shilay-Lee*
- Lt. Frederick Moore, killed in action—neck wound from enemy anti-aircraft shell
- Lt. Robert Barker, combat injury—burns from fire on the *Shilay-Lee*
- Sgt. Robert Jackson, killed in action when his combat damaged bomber crashed in the Adriatic Sea while struggling back to base
- T/Sgt Joseph Cutrone, combat injury—head injury from exploding anti-aircraft shell
- T/Sgt Wilburn Seal, combat injury—from enemy shrapnel after parachuting from the *Hearts and Flowers*

These airmen earned from three to five Oak Leaf Clusters each, and a few earned the Distinguished Flying Cross, including:

- Lt. Francis Boyle (posthumous)
- Lt. Frederick Moore (posthumous)
- Sgt. Wilburn Seal, planning and escaping from Bucharest POW camp
- Sgt. Wayne Simmons, rescuing airmen from a burning aircraft

Robert W. Simmons corresponded and remained in contact with his father's crew mates over the years. In a letter from James Benardini responding to Robert regarding facts about his father, T/Sgt. Wayne Simmons, Benardini stated:

> *"After we returned to Italy (from POW camp), Altvater, Barker and I were awarded the Purple Heart. Nothing was said why—we were all burned, and I had a back injury and facial burns."*

Responding to other questions posed by Robert Simmons, Benardini replied:

> *"No, Boyle didn't fly that day. He was injured when he was going into town in a jeep. We were not flying that (particular) day. Another aircraft going on a mission broke his nose gear, crashed...on fire at the end of the runway. That was just before the Regensburg flight—when we had a new pilot, Lt. Sparks, from Dayton, Ohio. He died in 1989.*
>
> *"I'm not sure, but Wayne (Simmons) probably got that (the Distinguished Flying Cross) for helping rescue people from the crashed aircraft. You might get better information from Chris (Christianson) or Bluhm. I wasn't with them (on that day)."*

Simmons and Bluhm acquired motorcycles—not exactly permitted by military regulations—which they used for transportation off base. They kept their 'bikes' stashed at the home of an Italian family that had befriended them. They may have motored to the crash site to help rescue the crew from their burning aircraft, because they arrived quickly enough to pull some to safety. Simmons described the horror of smelling the burning flesh to both his wife and young son as being the worst smell one could possibly experience.

A nice headstone marks the grave of Ova Wayne Simmons at the cemetery at Delhi, Oklahoma. There was insufficient space on his military footstone to include his Distinguished Flying Cross and Purple Heart citations; it's simply engraved:

OVA WAYNE SIMMONS
OKLAHOMA
T SGT ARMY AIR FORCES
WORLD WAR II A M & 5 OLC
MARCH 7 1924 SEPT 6 1956

Wilburn Seal, Simmons's cousin, is buried in a family plot in a beautiful cemetery at his hometown of Coleman, Texas. His gravestone is inscribed:

WILBURN WINIFRED SEAL
DEC 21 1923 AUG 24 1974
FATHER OF
AUDREY JEANETTE
FREDDY EDWIN
LARRY DON
DAVID NATHAN

The men of the *Hearts and Flowers*, the *Shilay-Lee*, and *Squeezie* stand among the greatest of American Heroes, giving credence to the term—*The Greatest Generation*.

What impact did the service and sacrifices of these twenty-four *Great American Heroes* have on us—the beneficiaries? Think about it—this is for you to decide.

ABOUT THE AUTHOR

Leon Cooper—retired educator, scientist and adventurer —was born in New Mexico eighteen years after statehood and grew up during the Great Depression and World War II.

He holds university degrees from Southern Nazarene University, University of Utah, and post-graduate studies at University of California-Berkeley and three other universities. He is an adventurer, musician, writer, aircraft pilot, inventor—the first to develop a three-dimensional photograph of a molecule, based on its electron probability distribution. Among his publications are:

Cooper, E. Leon, *The Electron Probability Distribution in Pi and Sigma Bonds of Carbon-like Molecules;* University of Utah and National Science Foundation, 1960.

Cooper, E. Leon, *Sistema Solar Hibridizado para el Secado de Legumbres en la Region Tropical del Chapare, Bolivia;* U.S. State Department and El Goberierno de Bolivia, 1983.

Cooper, E. Leon and DeLong, Deanna, *The Development of Persimmon Dehydration Processes in The Republic of Georgia;* ACDIVOCA, Republic of Georgia, 2004.

Cooper, Leon, *Water—A to Z;* Xlibris Corp., Philadelphia, Pennsylvania, 2005.

LEON COOPER

Mr. Cooper's professional experience includes teaching chemistry and physics, cyclotron and accelerator specialist at Los Alamos National Laboratory, and engineering applications across the Western Hemisphere and in Asia. He has traveled extensively and worked professionally around the world.

APPENDIX A

THIS PROJECT

What started out as a simple project more than a decade ago—to write a book about the sixty or so World War II veterans from my modest little community of Melrose, New Mexico—grew out of hand, literally exploding into a massive research into the lives and stories of scores upon scores of veterans who crossed paths with those whom I knew. The intent was to write a book of some two hundred pages, devoting three or four pages each to those who were from the Melrose community. One story led to another, then to another, until the simple project became a complex one. It soon became obvious that several volumes would be required to adequately articulate the stories of these veterans. As some of the accounts became intertwined with others, it was decided to group related stories into individual works. Since the inception of the project, extensive research has continued to provide additional background and information about World War II veterans.

The best and greatest source of information came from family members. I was fortunate in having numerous friends and acquaintances that assisted in collecting and providing stories, data and photos. It was a genuine privilege to meet with some of these veterans and their families—in Texas, Michigan, Oklahoma, and other states around the country and at home.

RESOURCES AND METHODOLOGY

The reader is encouraged to become actively involved in collecting, saving and disseminating the stories of those who served in World War II—and other wars—starting first with those individuals and/or their families. The Internet is another great source of information. It is advised to save the following Internet resource sites under *"Favorites"* or as *"Bookmarks"* in one's computer so that they're easily accessible for multiple searches.

One can *Google* a name (e.g., *stanley degeer*, *emory kemper*, etc...) and learn much (note: search engines don't recognize capitalized letters). Over time and through extensive 'surfing' of the Internet, numerous Web sites were located where accounts, data and photos may be found. Family members, however, constitute the best source of information for compiling a list of the crewmembers for a particular bomber or unit. For example, Wilburn Seal's daughter (Jeanette) provided her father's Bombardment Group ("463rd") and Squadron ("773rd") information. The *"463rd Bombardment Group"* Web site was located and found to contain all sorts of photos and information along with a 'bulletin board' through which one may interactively participate with others in sharing all sorts of valuable information. To visit that site, go to:

www.463rd.org

Leave a message, or post a question. Become a member. It's free.

The next step is to research the Internet. One first needs to determine the Air Force branch (e.g., *"8th Air Force"*, *"15th Air Force"*). Next, find the Bombardment Group (e.g., *"463rd"*, *"451st"*), followed by the Squadron (e.g., *"773rd"*, *"727th"*). After this information has been determined, it's a matter of surfing the Internet to locate specific, related Web sites where much can be found. One can also *Google* airplane types, such as *"p40"*, *"a26"*, or *"b25"*. One such database is located at:

http://www.b24.net/resrchrs/govlstings.htm

The federal government maintains numerous Web sites holding a wealth of data. Some of these sites are a bit tedious to navigate but, after a few trials and errors, one can locate and acquire a great deal of pertinent information. One such site, an archival treasure trove for researchers and genealogists alike, provides direct free access to individual military enlistment and service records for the years 1938–46, including prisoner of war records. Among the data is information regarding date of birth, enlistment date and place, nativity, branch of service, educational background, marital status and other valuable material. Prisoner of war records include the date of last report (missing), place of internment, date of repatriation, etc… This is an interactive Web site where one can type in whatever information that is known about a particular individual (i.e., *"bollei leo"* or *"seal wilburn")*, with the resulting page providing a dozen other pertinent pieces of information (i.e., *"enlistment at Sterling Heights, Michigan," "nativity, Michigan," "year, 1942,"* etc…). To visit this site, go to:

http://aad.archives.gov/aad/series

One of the most productive Web sites provides the source information for *MACR*s (Missing Air Crew Reports). From surfing through the previously mentioned Web sites and other sources, the *MACR* will have ordinarily appeared in one place or another. Once the correct *MACR* is determined, that particular document can be ordered. The *MACR* contains all the known information assembled at the time the aircraft went missing, including direct observations documented by members of other aircraft who witnessed what happened (i.e., *"…attacked head-on by a wall of Focke-Wulf fighters*; *…right engine on fire*; *…observed 7 parachutes*; *…spiraled downward to the right, exploded on impact…"*). The *MACR* also includes the identification of the aircraft, its armament, date and time of accident, name and rank of each crewmember, list of next of kin and other related information. The *MACRs* vary from five up to forty or more pages each, depending on what was learned at that time.

When ordering a particular *MACR*, one needs to provide the *MACR* number, if possible (e.g., *"5446", "5834"*). If the exact number is unknown, one can provide as much information as possible (e.g., *"date of accident," "country of accident," "type of aircraft"*).

Researchers living in the Washington, D.C. area actually extract and copy the reports from the archival data bases and send them by postal service. If those individuals have difficulty finding the exact *MACRs*, they will communicate through email in order to narrow down the exact reports. The charge for an *MACR* depends on how many pages are involved and usually costs around twenty to thirty dollars each. A week or more is usually required between the time of ordering and the receipt of the report. This site is located at:

http://www.aviationarcheaology.com/src/reports.htm

Sometimes it is important to determine where a particular individual resides. If he/she has a fairly common name (i.e., *"Jones"*, *"Smith"*, *"Taylor"*, etc…), it becomes somewhat difficult, because there may be five hundred *"Robert Joneses"* in the national telephone database. Knowing a middle initial (i.e., *"J"*, *"T"*, etc…) can further narrow the list to several dozen names. Then, determining the exact individual may depend on what is known about him/her, such as the state, county or town where he/she may have lived. A free white pages database is located at:

http://www.whitepages.com/9900/

One may wish to determine whether a particular individual is living. In this case, check for that individual's name in the Social Security Death Index (*"SSDI"*). This free database provides information regarding date of birth, date of death, place of death and other useful data. One need only fill in the information online, including last name, first name and initial (if known), using the "simple" search. If other information is known (i.e., date and/or place of birth, date and/or place of death, or other bits of data), then the "advanced" search option should be used. This site is located at:

http://ssdi.rootsweb.ancestry.com/

Good Hunting!

APPENDIX B

15TH AIR FORCE BOMBER GROUPS & SQUADRONS

B-17 GROUPS—SQUADRONS

- 002nd BG—20th, 49th, 96th, 429th BS
- 097th BG—340th, 341st, 342nd, 414th BS
- 099th BG—346th, 347th, 348th, 416th BS
- 301st BG—32nd, 352nd, 353rd, 354th, 419th BS
- 463rd BG—772nd, 773rd, 774th, 775th BS
- 483rd BG—815th, 816th, 817th, 840th BS

B-24 GROUPS—SQUADRONS

- 098th BG—343rd, 344th, 345th, 415th BS
- 376th BG—512th, 513th, 514th, 515th BS
- 449th BG—716th, 717th, 718th, 719th BS
- 450th BG—720th, 721st, 722nd, 723rd BS
- 451st BG—724th, 725th, 726th, 727th BS
- 454th BG—736th, 737th, 738th, 739th BS
- 455th BG—740th, 741st, 742nd, 743rd BS
- 456th BG—744th, 745th, 746th, 747th BS
- 459th BG—756th, 757th, 758th, 759th BS

LEON COOPER

- 460th BG—760th, 761st, 762nd, 763rd BS
- 461st BG—764th, 765th, 766th, 767th BS
- 464th BG—776th, 777th, 778th, 779th BS
- 465th BG—780th, 781st, 782nd, 783rd BS
- 484th BG—824th, 825th, 826th, 827th BS
- 485th BG—828th, 829th, 830th, 831st BS

APPENDIX C

15TH AIR FORCE BOMBER LOSSES

ON MAY 5, 1944—PLOESTI MISSION

SERIAL	TYPE	BG-BS	MACR
42-52094	B-24	451-	4604
42-30072	B-17	097-342	4607
42-50307	B-24	449-719	4608 "Bonnie's Boys"
42-31796	B-17	463-774	4623
42-52149	B-24	449-718	4661 Big Nose from KY"
42-52260	B-24	455-	4662
42-64394	B-24	449-717	4665 Miss Bea Haven"
41-29512	B-24	449-716	4667 "Troop Sleeper"
42-97583	B-17	463-774	4712
42-52222	B-24	456-746	4713
42-07744	B-24	449-717	4714 "Shack Happy"
42-64499	B-24	456-745	4749
41-29239	B-24	451-727	5446 "Shilay-Lee"

15ᵀᴴ AIR FORCE BOMBER LOSSES
ON MAY 18, 1944—PLOESTI MISSION

SERIAL	TYPE	BG-SQ	MACR
42-41257	B-24	011-234	4683
42-97726	B-17	463-772	4816
42-78081	B-24	455-	4842
42-52253	B-24	455-	4843
42-52355	B-24	460-	5044
41-29576	B-24	459-	5048
42-64347	B-24	455-	5057
42-52170	B-24	449-	5060
42-97540	B-17	463-775	5061
42-106991	B-17	099-347	5066
41-28246	B-24	454-	5067
42-31829	B-17	463-772	5434
42-31826	B-17	463-775	5791
42-52351	B-24	459-	5830
42-31803	B-17	463-	5832
42-31791	B-17	463-773	5834 "Hearts&Flowers"

APPENDIX D

AMERICAN POWS HELD IN RUMANIA
(971 OF 1,127 POWS IDENTIFIED)

Serial#	Name(Last First Initial)	USA	Camp
32557890	Abbink Joseph E	NJ	46-26
35560951	Abel Richard E	IN	49-11
O&697762	Abrams, Solomon E	SC	45-21
O&763886	Aclin Lloyd B	AR	
34313483	Adcock Edgar H	VA	45-21
12125211	Ahrensfeldt Louis H	NY	
32176780	Aiello William J	NY	45-21
O&857919	Ainsworth Ernest F		45-21
O&682271	Allaire Edward J	TX	45-21
17966830	Allen Gillman C	IL	45-21
24686935	Allen James T	GA	45-21
38424897	Allen Joseph H		45-21
38467062	Allinder James H	OK	45-21
O&688734	Alsdorf Albert J	IA	49-11
O1284977	Althouse James G	OH	45-21
O&688491	Altvater Julius A	NJ	45-21
O&716615	Ames Paul V		45-21
O&688896	Amster Louis	NJ	45-21
39836544	Ancheta Tranquilino	CA	

Serial#	Name(Last First Initial)	USA	Camp
O&694294	Anderson Howard J	NY	45-21
O&753045	Anderson Albert W	NY	45-21
O&808336	Anderson Edwin O	MN	45-21
O&760525	Anderson George A	IA	45-21
O&691858	Anderson Patrick J	OH	45-21
13157436	Angell John C	PA	45-21
39695342	Angeloni Joseph E		45-21
18170541	Antilley Milton L	LA	45-21
O&686175	Armistead Lewis A	MA	45-21
36739550	Armstrong Garland L	IL	45-21
O&793973	Aronson Albert M	SC	45-21
38141408	Arrington Rozell D		45-21
11053561	Asadorian Charles G	MA	54-16
O&819664	Asbury Thomas G	NC	45-21
17099906	Atchison William H	KS	45-21
O&684828	Athenas Joseph E	NJ	45-21
T&001434	Atkins Joseph E	NC	45-21
14151747	Atkinson James C	MS	45-21
O&811309	Austin Norman D	WI	45-21
31218942	Austin Ralph W	ME	45-21
12208603	Babcock Roy A	NY	
O&704869	Badger Thomas C		45-21
O&691468	Bahti Lenus A	MN	
15339989	Bailey Aronold A	WV	45-21
3801746	Bailey George E	OK	
13083742	Bailey Wallace E	PA	
36573760	Baker Roy L	MI	
35874291	Baldwin Kenneth P	KY	
39904078	Ballard Eugene H	UT	
O&07505	Ballard Wallace B	TX	
17129455	Bantz Clinton D	KS	

Serial#	Name(Last First Initial)	USA	Camp
32751347	Bard Herman L	NJ	
O&716699	Barker John R	NY	
O&690347	Barker Robert J	NJ	
O&814849	Barmore Robert K	NJ	
O7701997	Barney Kenneth D	KS	
32874730	Bartfeld Harvey		45-21
33179524	Barton Harry J		45-21
13080216	Basquill John J Jr	PA	
34851021	Batten Willie M		45-21
32365561	Baumeister Frank		45-21
O7413562	Beane James B	CA	
37611309	Beasley Jesse E		45-21
35339987	Beers William, C	OH	
O&747567	Bell Edward W	NJ	
18215813	Bell Jordan F	TX	
15010864	Benardini James N	OH	45-21
18128123	Bennett J D	TX	54-16
O1691670	Bennett John D		45-21
O8691608	Berg Robert J	NY	
32716260	Bergmann Arthur E	NY	
1613954	Bernstein Jerrold S	IL	
32321529	Berry Loyd G	NY	
35770956	Betz William F	OH	
7030655	Bevil Orbie G		45-21
39022462	Beyerle Peter J	CA	
17073824	Biggerstaff Robert E	IL	
34202986	Bindrim Arthur J	FL	49-11
37413730	Bishop Alex E	MO	
13094871	Bistline Charles R	PA	
35468607	Black Paul M		45-21
T&121895	Blanchard Keller	LA	

Serial#	Name(Last First Initial)	USA	Camp
35337852	Blanchard William H	IN	
O&399650	Blehm Harold E	CO	
36425486	Bluhm Robert M	IL	
32422274	Blum Raymond D	NY	
32597073	Boccino Thomas G		45-21
O&811526	Bodwell Richard K Jr	NH	
O&688903	Boffa Victor M	PA	
31371559	Bohn Abraham		45-21
O&808937	Bollei Leo	IL	
16049892	Bond Harris L		45-21
O&818533	Bonetti Frank L	PA	
O&808351	Boone George B	NY	
34395963	Boren Earl E Jr	AL	
34430879	Borland James C	NC	
19111995	Borrows William R	WA	
O&755509	Botkin John E	CA	
31266010	Bowes Maurice E	NH	
39089906	Boyet Elzer R	CA	45-21
O&690621	Boyle Glen E	IL	
35092672	Boyle James J Jr		45-21
O&752311	Brannon Richard E	OH	
O&716707	Braun William R	OH	45-21
O&697389	Brawninger Earl W	OH	
O&806044	Brazier Harold W	NY	
31120981	Brazzale Guido N		45-21
O&683810	Breeding Eugene B	VA	
O&814236	Brennan William J	PA	
18117261	Brewer Charlie P	TX	
O&755271	Briggs Gerald A	OR	
38294170	Briggs John H Jr	AR	
15330350	Brioli Amarico J	IN	

Serial#	Name(Last First Initial)	USA	Camp
O&808360	Bristor, William B		45-21
13157945	Brlansky Joseph C	PA	49-11
31072369	Brock Harry A	MA	
O&802986	Bronstein Harvey W	MA	
O&713108	Brooks Richard C	IL	
O&702226	Brotherton Charles R		45-21
O&806205	Brown Lawrence J	VT	45-21
15174110	Brown Sidney E	WV	
12203829	Brunton Frank R	NJ	
32383384	Brusso Robert F	NY	
O&751092	Buckmaster Duane M	IA	
18038224	Buckner Roy W		45-21
O&757458	Buckwalter Robert M	CA	
18061547	Buffington Edward A	TX	
O&747637	Burczak Stanley P	IN	
33409074	Burke William A	PA	
16128894	Burnett Howard	IL	
13109705	Burrows Donald C	PA	
	Buschard Bernard J	MO	
18167903	Butler William J	IA	
O&701559	Buzzard Ross N	TX	
33609844	Byer Robert P	PA	
32893902	Byzek Hyman G	NY	
O&749582	Cadwallader S H Jr	PA	
T&121944	Cady Raymond I	DC	
34084707	Cagle Hubert R	GA	
35723044	Cahill Leslie A	IN	43-27
O&378451	Call George W	TX	
32892514	Call Ira M	NY	
13098240	Camillo Calvin H	PA	
T&162487	Cantrell Everett E		45-21

Serial#	Name(Last First Initial)	USA	Camp
19085573	Carberry Robert J	CA	54-16
33419808	Carik William	PA	
19159294	Carmignani George		45-21
16138058	Carmody Edward G	IL	45-21
T&123219	Carr Rudolph C		45-21
O1695418	Carr Rudolph C	KY	
O1691689	Carr Sidney R		45-21
34598720	Carroll David E	NC	
16094842	Carroll Patrick M	WI	
34504800	Carson Doyle C	TN	
14138258	Carter Lucious	FL	
17071948	Cassidy William L	MO	
11106217	Cassinelli Albert	MA	45-21
11041564	Chadwick P A Jr	CT	
38453144	Chafin Billy J	TX	45-21
T&125268	Chajka Paul R	OH	
36814073	Chambers David R	CA	
O&695037	Cheesman Robert E	IL	
34524527	Chessor Samuel J	MI	
37453435	Child Kenneth R		45-21
15062996	Childress James W Jr	KY	
39106733	Chinn Henry C	CA	54-16
16078368	Chinn Lynn S	MO	
35316102	Chonka John	OH	
11131552	Chretien Robert J	MA	
O&808782	Christian Vernon A	TX	
37323811	Christianson Allen G	MN	
32709399	Chused Louis	NY	
32738825	Clark John J		45-21
O&703702	Clark Joseph D Jr	IL	

Serial#	Name(Last First Initial)	USA	Camp
15333662	Clark William G	KY	
35591399	Clatterbuck Drexel W	OH	
39035056	Claverie Leon M	CA	
O1703116	Clay Robert J	CA	
69455689	Clement Warren G	WV	
17969117	Cline Floyd W	IA	
O&713128	Coates Richard A		45-21
12168032	Cobb Thomas C		45-21
O&810828	Cocking Byron D	PA	43-27
O&693972	Cole Bertram E		45-21
34074954	Colley Demcey D		
31279944	Collins Frederick H	CN	
12037239	Collum Charles E	NY	49-11
32754511	Comegys William G	DE	45-11
O&752841	Concidine William	CA	
34685937	Conner James N		45-21
15106184	Conrad Frederick J		45-21
O&707175	Conway Henry A		45-21
36742442	Conway Virgil E		45-21
13044832	Cooke Edwin J	PA	45-21
O&683971	Copeland Sam H	TX	45-21
O&677447	Coppedge Jess	WA	45-21
O&703609	Cordery Edmund P	NJ	45-21
O&690628	Constantino Michael	OH	45-21
O&692300	Courtin Jack W	OH	46-26
12122236	Cowan Julian V	NY	#07244 A C
O&814255	Cowgill Winfield P	NJ	45-21
O&812226	Cox Fritz L	AL	45-21
O&812226	Cox James P	NC	
O&679609	Crans Russell K	PA	54-12

Serial#	Name(Last First Initial)	USA	Camp
33522388	Cratch Albert E	VA	45-21
O&703711	Cress Robert W	IL	45-21
29519922	Creviston John L		45-21
31089525	Cronin Austin J	MA	49-11
32279285	Cronin James P	NJ	45-21
15108377	Crouch Rayond	IL	45-21
O&811343	Crumbliss Jack A	TX	45-21
12038841	Cuff Eugene	NJ	45-21
14181033	Culler Bufort E	NC	54-16
18169319	Culver Robert B Jr	MO	45-21
O&747378	Currie Julian E	MS	45-21
38324986	Curtis Chase Y	OR	45-21
32721353	Cutrone Joseph J	NY	45-21
O&757423	Czajkowski George J	IL	45-21
16168266	Czerwinski Wm. V	IL	45-21
O&690780	Dailey Judson L	OH	
O&750953	Dallas Alexander S	OH	
O&695884	Daniels George D	TX	
18161336	Danielson Carl G	OK	
35417691	Danison Gerald V	OH	
39127414	Davis Ben W	CA	54-16
39279362	Davis Otis V	CA	45-21
O&755147	Dawson Thomas J	MS	
O&735286	De Rudder Peter J	IL	
O&761901	Dean Bob L	OH	
T&125065	Decker Frederick C		45-21
O&811578	Decosta Joseph J	NY	
18187521	Delaney Olan	TX	45-21
O&688933	Demas William	IL	
O&810633	Denham Charles R	MO	
O&818121	Dennis Richard M	NY	

Serial#	Name(Last First Initial)	USA	Camp
35622726	Deringer George A	OH	
36024888	Despain Glen P	IA	49-11
O&743571	Devereux James J		45-21
O&690637	Devlin Joseph L	PA	
12183914	Dickwisch Reinhard	NY	
12215199	Dimaggio John J	NY	
31281196	Diminno Adolph J	CT	
13044779	Diviney John F	PA	
17040410	Dobb George F		45-21
36461680	Dolbee Harold S		45-21
15323567	Domoracki John C	OH	
O&818643	Donad James C	NJ	
32726746	Donnelly Thomas B	NY	49-11
O&808966	Donner, John B	MI	49-11
O&816646	Douthwright David L	MA	43-27
33529603	Doyle Henry J	X	45-21
O&797492	Dragner Thomas J Jr	X	45-21
15047363	Drane Leroy M	X	45-21
O&811182	Draut George A	X	45-21
O&805316	Drutman Nathaniel	NY	
O&748378	Dugi August H	TX	
O&697481	Dunbar Gerald K	WI	
O&813348	Duncan Robert A		45-21
18187403	Dunderdale Ottis W	TX	
O&812234	Dunham John N		45-21
O&698182	Dunn Jackson F	NC	
O&698182	Dunn John F	MA	
368221269	Duren James S		45-21
O&753070	Dyer Harold E	CA	
38464873	Edwards Carl D	X	45-21
O&735546	Egan John T Jr	TX	

Serial#	Name(Last First Initial)	USA	Camp
O&754897	Egbert Harold H	NY	
36432430	Eggemeyer Victor H	IL	45-21
O*723327	Ehrenfeld Sherwood	NY	
O&692541	Eley William B	VA	45-21
O&686529	Elliott Gerald B	TX	
16151895	Engel Frederick G	MI	45-21
O&691249	Ennis Richard J	WA	
16042830	Eschbach Donald L	MI	
11131604	Espinola Lionel F		45-21
O&755176	Evenson Melvin	MN	
19125124	Evenson Romaine K	MT	
O&698186	Fagan John F		45-21
O&706720	Failor Lloyd E	OH	
O&687824	Falvo Louis	PA	
O&695361	Faris James E Jr	VA	
14161846	Farrell J L Jr	TN	49-11
33286674	Fasolas Charles E	PA	46-26
O&704121	Fayard Fred E Jr	MS	
39555339	Fernandez Renee	CA	
38370393	Fidler Jackson H	TX	
13151977	Fili William J	PA	
O&699050	Filkorn Harry	OH	
19203089	Finkelstein Max M	CA	
O&669261	Finley Morris E	OK	
18061000	Fisher Frank A	VA	
T&061539	Fisher Sidney	NY	
35576200	Fisher Theodore R		45-21
O&817648	Fitz Elwood A	OH	
O&818569	Fitzgerald James J	MI	48-11
15332826	Fitzpatrick Clark S Jr	IN	45-21
O&701586	Flynn Joseph P	MA	

Serial#	Name(Last First Initial)	USA	Camp
32863848	Foden Kenneth G	NY	
O&686688	Fogel Anthony	NY	
31325451	Foley William J	CT	
O&807406	Fonteneau Richard A	VT	
O&826129	Foor Herbert L	IN	
O&757803	Foppinno Leslie F	CA	49-11
O&690644	Forshage Felix C	TX	
20454253	Foster Alson B	NC	
35283693	Foster Daniel E	OH	
39121479	Foster John G	CA	45-21
	Fowler George E	CA	
O&674749	Fox Irving H	NY	
15070191	Franco John F	OH	45-21
12049702	Frank Edward W	NJ	45-21
O&694443	Franks James R	AL	
O&820652	Frazier Paul D	OH	48-11
O&763150	Freestone Earl G	AZ	
33626413	Fritz Harry B		45-21
11008547	Fugere Lucien G	MA	
37521338	Fulton Harold D	KS	
O&735563	Funk Glenferd E	KS	
12093100	Gaghan John E	NJ	
O&748065	Gall James W	MA	45-21
31151569	Galland Alfred J	ME	
32761046	Galvin John J	NJ	
16143427	Gamache Harold J	IL	
O&750570	Garrity Joseph A	WI	
O&691983	Gavora John Jr	NJ	43-27
12136576	Gaynor Harry		45-11
33765633	Gdula Michael E		45-11
39292047	Gerken Gilbert E	CA	

Serial#	Name(Last First Initial)	USA	Camp
O&748958	Geyman Ranomd J	IN	
33367467	Giambrone William J	PA	
O&702409	Gibbs Roy W	NE	
O&696084	Giles Willard J Jr	GA	
O&690406	Ginder Willard R Jr	PA	43-27
15377718	Gittery Vernon H	OH	
O&741507	Gladstone Abner B	NJ	
O&709473	Gloeckner Ernest V	NY	
37374559	Godwin Harold T	MO	45-21
18181294	Goodman Jimmy E	TX	
13023454	Goodman Saul D	MD	
20346864	Goodwin France L Jr	MD	
O&752331	Gottlieb Stanley I	NY	
18156755	Graf Eugene	TX	
T&001688	Grammens Leon T	MI	
34700066	Gray Jack D	AL	49-11
O&462381	Gray James S	NC	
12017792	Graziano Joseph	NY	
O&703241	Green Benoni S	IL	
39694599	Green John A	CA	
17035296	Green Wilbur C	IL	54-16
35567251	Greene Lawrence L	IN	
O&707385	Greenfeder Herbert	NJ	
36440777	Greer Bert E	IL	
33540868	Griffin Willard E	VA	
16055084	Griffith Kenneth	IL	
34720268	Grubbs Garland F	TN	
O&766367	Gubler Edmund V	NV	
O&690212	Guynes Joseph B	TX	
O&419224	Haas Chester R		45-21
36480722	Hagen Louis W		45-21

Serial#	Name(Last First Initial)	USA	Camp
O&682028	Hagenson Eugene G	IA	
O&685118	Hager Jack L	OH	
O&752617	Hale Edmond C	MI	
O&689502	Hall Arthur T	NY	
35319111	Hall Robert E	WV	45-21
39858914	Hall Ronald E	AZ	
32581654	Hammer Arthur R		45-21
T&123538	Hammerberg Jack L	CA	
O&692549	Hampton James B	CA	
19112105	Haney Jack R	WA	
13120901	Haney Randolph F	VA	
37413752	Hankins Irwin M	MO	
O&811898	Hanson David G	NJ	
O&820007	Hardin William		45-21
20818855	Harding Walard J	TX	
12168296	Hardy Robert R	PA	
16079794	Hare Jack F		45-21
O&702273	Harn Hugh L	IA	45-21
O&412729	Harper Henry A	IA	45-21
O&811902	Harper Joseph W	WV	45-21
39270270	Harrell Samuel	CA	45-21
38369452	Harris Harry B	TX	
13078330	Hartman John E	PA	45-21
19101496	Hartman John T	CA	45-21
32712013	Hartung Warren G	NY	
37506265	Haskins Ferd A	MO	45-21
O&663919	Hassey Lindley P		45-21
O&701598	Hastings Theodore F		45-21
16126363	Hauf Leroy M	IL	
15324809	Haught Howard L	WV	
19140320	Haumann Martin Jr	CA	

Serial#	Name(Last First Initial)	USA	Camp
O&684864	Haun Charles R	MI	43-27
T&123753	Hawkins Charles M	X	45-21
15112640	Hawkins Charles S	KY	
O&683929	Hawkins Herbert C Jr		45-21
14151502	Hayman Bennie C	MS	45-21
O&755686	Hebert James P Jr	LA	
36601627	Hein Edward J	IL	
39697534	Heisler Paul L		45-21
34767355	Henderson Berry D	GA	
34601337	Henderson W A Jr	NC	45-21
36816139	Hendricks Lewis R	WI	54-16
13099707	Henry Thomas M	PA	45-21
13145872	Hepler Arnold W	PA	
32592282	Herres Francis J	NJ	
36457489	Hettinga Martin Jr	MI	43-27
13076063	Higginbotham A P	MD	
11117116	Hill Elton J	MA	
T&186254	Hill James L		45-21
19055765	Hippe Ingmar A	ND	45-21
O&749776	Hirsch Milton J	NY	
O&759003	Hisey Ralph W Jr	OH	45-21
O&732247	Hodgson Thomas D	CA	
O&755563	Hoffman Marvin E	CA	45-21
20620471	Hogan Robert E	IL	54-16
O&663616	Hoggatt Robert A	IL	45-21
O&812994	Holgate William R	WI	
O&811646	Hollerbach Raymond	MI	45-21
O&772117	Hollingshead H K Jr	IA	
37394640	Holt James T	MO	
O&822441	Holt John M	TX	
15394246	Honaker Charles E	WV	

Serial#	Name(Last First Initial)	USA	Camp
13132305	Hoobler Harold E		45-21
14156372	Hooper Roy C		45-21
34476553	Hoover Otho	MS	
16088263	Hopper Mitchell C	MI	
13094696	Hostetter Frank B		45-21
18162258	Howard Oren E	OK	45-21
32874356	Hucke Herman R	NY	45-21
O&699419	Hudson Guy L		45-21
12002681	Hughes Walter E		45-21
19017427	Huhnke Robert E	WA	45-21
33719186	Hull John D	MD	
15406187	Humphrey Charles E	IN	
O&681893	Hunt Robert P	SD	
O&663919	Hussey Lindley P	AZ	
14160697	Igou James M	TN	
14132504	Ingram John W	TN	
O&689528	Iusi John G	PA	
O&421106	Jackson Elwin H	OK	
O&01606	Jacobs Morris E	CO	
O&749252	Jacobson Roy L	MN	
O&694557	James Willard L	UT	
35600956	Jarrard John H	PA	
O&885560	Jefferson William H	WI	
11045451	Jenkins Harold V	CT	
O&742427	Jenkins Robert L	CA	
39268112	Jensen Leslie M	CA	
37441490	Jensen Roland T H	IA	
O&688704	Jerolaman Donald W	DC	
39277207	Jespersen Woodrow	CA	54-16
O&690439	Johannsen Glenn F	IA	
37415622	Johnson Foy B	MO	

Serial#	Name(Last First Initial)	USA	Camp
33434907	Johnson Paul E	PA	
O&678533	Johnson Robert E	IL	
O&690440	Johnson Roy E	GA	
O&756249	Johnson Roy W	CA	
O&698721	Jolley William H Jr	TN	
34625074	Jolly Murray O	MS	
15338967	Jordan James M	OH	
6480126	Junge Paul F	IL	
O&696102	Kamps Everett C	NY	48-11
O&695666	Karlovitz William F	IL	
O&804348	Kendall Richard W	IN	
18108081	Kenreigh John D	OK	49-11
33357229	Kessler Jacob R	NY	
O&684343	Kessling Walter R	IA	
16076479	Kibler Bert E	IA	
O&735397	Kill Joseph F	IL	
	Killer Bert E	IL	
19079370	Kimzey Dexter E	WY	
O&698891	King Oliver H	TX	
O&687862	Kinne Warren H	NJ	
14160457	Kirby Claude E	TN	
O&680455	Kitson Francis	OH	
39680056	Kittelson Lloyd K	MN	
T&123677	Kline George E	PA	
O&690582	Kline Richard C	CA	
34776302	Knuckles James D	NC	
32080930	Kochnover Stanley	NY	
31265697	Kodet Edward	SD	
15105702	Koenigseker Aaron L	OH	
O&719098	Koponen Melvin E	MI	
34503266	Kourvelas Charles P	TN	

Serial#	Name(Last First Initial)	USA	Camp
O&747434	Krueger Paul E	IL	
36501363	Krug Angus L	MI	
O&756997	Krushat Warren S	CA	
31286865	Krzeminski John J	MA	
37208899	Laclef Densal E	KS	43-27
O&683724	Lahr Paul A	PA	
O&752818	Langpop Louis G	IL	
17060075	Lannon Louis A	MO	43-27
16088509	Lanphear William H	MI	
O&693335	Laughlin William M	CA	
15018351	Laver EdwardJr	OH	
17127701	Lawless Elmer N	MO	
O&708498	Lee John E	PA	
O&399672	Leggat George W	MI	
O&745122	Lehner Albert M	WA	
O&811099	Leins John A	IN	
38395045	Lemke Vernon W	OK	
32388019	Levin Sidney J	NJ	
38087501	Lewis Chester A	TX	
O&713198	Liebl Howard C	NY	
O&675243	Lindley Bennie B	TX	
O&737159	Lindus Milden A	OH	
19002136	Linhares Carl J	CA	43-27
O&023300	Litton William P	MS	
38463290	Livesay Gerald R	OK	43-27
11085542	Lizotte Robert A	VT	43-27
38103820	Lobato Eulalio B	NM	
O&740848	Lockhart John L	WA	
35497647	Loge Merlin A	IN	
O&690125	Lombardi James C	MA	
33459769	Loomis Elwin L	PA	

LEON COOPER

Serial#	Name(Last First Initial)	USA	Camp
O&752689	Lorber Marvin	NY	
6248234	Louthan John H	CO	
34763512	Love James R	GA	
O&735410	Love William F	CA	
7000835	Lowe Jesse Q	MS	
36195623	Lozinski Joseph J	IL	
11094770	Luscinskas Frank W	CT	
O&700638	Luttrell Guy A	MD	
O&695678	Lyga Michael	NJ	
39193545	Lyke Richard G	WA	49-11
O&735091	Lyles John F	FL	49-11
O&799596	Lyman Edward M	VA	
O&691399	Lynch Charles R	ID	
35600622	Lynch Frank W	OH	
O&687200	Lynn Robert E	MO	
O&689619	MacDonald Bertell A	WI	
O&667086	MacDonald Donald J	ND	49-11
O&755382	MacDonell Donald G	MN	
19172151	MacNeil Vernon R	ID	45-21
O&354961	MacQueen Henry C	WV	
O&685676	Mack Arthur W	OH	
OY690959	Madorin Frederick L	IL	
16156435	Mahuta Eugene A	WI	
32672283	Majchrzak Harry J	NY	45-25
31267770	Major Robert R	NH	
32489674	Makanowitsky Paul	NY	
O&707294	Malone Robert P	MA	
2765739	Maloney Bernard J	NJ	
O&807497	Mamiotka Anthony J	PA	
32738591	Mann James E	NY	
19099456	Mansfield William J	CA	

Serial#	Name(Last First Initial)	USA	Camp
O&801185	Marioles Peter S	FL	
37144445	Marnell Patrick A	KS	48-15
O&462279	Marquith Malcolm	NY	
32488504	Marshall Joseph L	DE	
38462930	Marshall Rufas W	TX	
O&685006	Martin Joseph	MA	
18193840	Martin Rudolph A	OK	
O&814509	Martim William C Jr	OK	
O&807485	Masneri Robert	PA	
36425682	Massa John B	IL	
19056354	Massey Loren W	CA	
O&695370	Matney Arlo R	MI	
37319608	Mattern John	ND	49-11
O&700619	Mattingly Edwin J	MO	
12134719	May Alan R	NJ	
32114264	Mayer Charles P	NJ	
T&062052	McAuliffe John H	MA	
O&699523	McCabe William F	NY	
O&681449	McCormick John M	IN	
19143688	McCormick Robert J	WA	
O&689481	McCoy Kenneth B	IN	
O&738720	McCrary Edwin	GA	
37045477	McDonald George P	IA	45-21
O&754400	McDonnell Edward J	NY	
13112372	McDowell Donald J	PA	
16151592	McDowell Harry	MI	
O&701619	McElwain Leo	KS	
18200403	McGlaun Donald E	TX	
O&699219	McIntosh William A	NY	
O&689317	McInturff Ben	OK	
12080312	McKinley George	NY	

Serial#	Name(Last First Initial)	USA	Camp
O&813465	McManmon Leo J	NY	
34645764	McMillan J P Jr	SC	
O&753699	McMonegal John P	PA	
17097168	McMurray John P	IA	
18201430	McMurtre Newman	TX	43-27
O&701493	McShane Edward J	PA	
11096528	McTiernan John L	MA	
O&743465	McWilliams Victor	IL	
34704030	Meacham Charles T	AL	
O&697896	Mee Frederick C	CA	
O&816340	Meehan Patrick J Jr	PA	
O&700111	Meers Alvin W	IL	45-20
17164580	Merkel Donald L	NE	
O&668728	Merriell Franklin M	OH	
33460041	Merrill Clayton L	PA	49-11
39035077	Merritt Earl L	CA	
12073039	Messina Paul V	NY	
32712054	Meyer John J Jr	NY	
O&757011	Meyer R B	TX	
16033385	Meyers Harold J	IL	
38414180	Mhoon Robert J	TX	
35651575	Millar Douglas M	WV	45-21
33248554	Miller Newell L	PA	45-21
38266458	Miller William H	LA	
O&752069	Mills Thomas A	IN	
T&124862	Minasian Mike T	MI	
O&406601	Minervini Robert H	OH	
O&742509	Minor Lancelot		
33117047	Moffet Donald W	PA	
34604201	Montague Robert L	NC	
13045914	Moore Hugh M	PA	45-21

Serial#	Name(Last First Initial)	USA	Camp
O&704226	Moore Joel R	ID	
33225043	Moore John J Jr	VA	
O&682711	Moore Orville S	IN	
14165966	Morgan Dwight T	NC	
39294393	Morledge Jack C	CA	
19048981	Morrell Douglas W	NE	
35758710	Morris Dale	WV	45-21
12126957	Morris John J	NY	
13136200	Morrison George W	WV	
O&804381	Morton Alfred C	VA	
35696935	Moser Clarence A	IN	
O&822512	Moses Elias E	PA	
32691334	Mroczkowski M J	NY	
O&814732	Mueller Edward L	OH	
11998897	Muffat Robert B	SD	
O&713212	Mullen George N	MI	
O&705411	Murphy Robert M Jr	TN	43-27
31101905	Murphy Thomas J	CT	
O&818195	Murphy Walter A	PA	
O&750819	Murray Arthur E	NJ	
32723364	Muzii Louis A	NY	
33082304	Myers Michael	PA	43-27
33599431	Myles David Jr	PA	
O&687623	Myllmaki Edward E	MA	
18033663	Myrick Troy E	TX	
O&807497	Namiotka Anthony J	PA	
18209685	Nelson Delbert E	LA	43-27
14129166	Nelson Fuller E	GA	
O&812295	Nelson Robert L	PA	
32762877	Nepil Slavomir		45-21
O&716670	Nesbit Donald D	CA	

Serial#	Name(Last First Initial)	USA	Camp
O&685700	Newsom Robert L	IN	43-27
37527437	Newton Thelbert L	MO	
O&704130	Nixon George F	CA	
35442285	Nolin Albert E	IL	48-15
O&760372	Noone Harry E	MO	
O&424125	Norgard Clifford D	NE	
O&752074	Nosal John	NJ	
32770916	Nuber Roland A		45-21
O&807775	Oakes Ralph Q	CA	
O&810934	Odle Clarence B	OH	43-27
35551092	Okapal John A	OH	
6960139	Oneal James A	TX	
39551615	Openshaw Melvin L	CA	45-21
19149689	Orrico Charles J		45-21
34613566	Owen David B Jr	NC	
34603622	Owen Willie R Jr	NC	
O&689634	Paglieri Charles M	NY	
O&755748	Paradise William	NY	
O&689986	Pardue Robert L	TX	
35792727	Parker Eugene Jr	OH	54-16
O&667099	Paar James H	TX	
O&700049	Patterson Wallace S		45-21
33871548	Paul Albert Ira	PA	
33610024	Pawloski Edmund L	PA	
37539417	Pearce Albert L		45-21
16169851	Peccia Alfred A		45-21
38385213	Peck Milton H	LA	
O&801568	Petrokovich Walter	ME	
O&801568	Philbin James P	MI	45-21
36432087	Phillips Robert D	IL	
O&698142	Pieper Donald J	IL	

Serial#	Name(Last First Initial)	USA	Camp
O&672666	Pinson Charles H		45-21
62699354	Pinter Alfred T	TX	
O&684892	Pluim Peter	CA	
16113337	Pociecha Raymond	CA	
37232244	Poffinberger Ralph L	MO	
36477244	Pogue Bernard N	IL	
35752207	Poling Ralph W	MD	45-21
O663173	Polink Anthony D	PA	
O&698226	Poore Wesley A	IA	43-27
O&669920	Porter John E		45-21
35765816	Pospieszynski Thadd	OH	45-21
31198093	Potvin Alexic V	CT	
17112243	Powell Elvin G		45-21
17128724	Powers Donnie E	KS	
16143400	Preihs Russell H	IL	
32889877	Prian Joseph D	NY	54-16
O&700766	Prophater Raymond		45-21
	Pulman Rudolph J	IL	
14056753	Pyatte Wade E	NC	54-16
O&551059	Pyle William H		45-21
11116394	Pyne Arthur R		45-21
32878885	Pyzanowski Frank J	NY	48-15
18190535	Rabe Willard A	TX	
O&689649	Ralston Robert B	PA	
33505411	Rank Glen A	PA	
32744829	Reader Edward J	NY	
32735394	Reichardt Paul S	NY	54-16
13151695	Rendelman Joseph A	PA	
O&691291	Rhoades John J	MO	
O&691918	Rice Paul G	FL	
O&684813	Rickey Ralph R	OK	

Serial#	Name(Last First Initial)	USA	Camp
01168049	Riddle Dennis R		45-21
32276301	Rifinsky Joseph V	NJ	
O&737250	Ring Charles B Jr		45-21
16051463	Ringenberg Earl E	IL	
35532545	Risch Burdell C		45-15
O&816588	Rittenhouse W H Hr	AL	
39282253	Roark Howard	CA	
O&743285	Robbins William S	WI	
35490909	Robertson Dallis R		
O&024769	Robinson Floyd I	IN	
32773719	Roehr Henry J	NJ	
O&749323	Rogers Dale E	KS	46-26
36739551	Rogers Edward A		45-21
O&821782	Roper John		45-21
O&696149	Roseberg Carl G Jr	CA	45-21
35725180	Rose Leonard E	IN	54-16
O&699248	Ross Harley H	OH	45-21
O&755196	Roth Martin E	NY	
320199143	Rothenburg George F	CT	
31220209	Roy Robert L		45-21
21128287	Rurak Phillip A	MA	45-21
31285389	Ryan Timothy J Jr		45-21
32741092	Ryan William J	NY	45-21
32452166	Sagis Victor R	NJ	
11168586	Salovitz Irwin		45-21
33191470	Salter Frank R	DC	
33432237	Salyards Glenn A		45-21
O&696152	Samms Marshall N	NJ	
17128289	Samuels Harry C	KS	
37065094	Sanders James Q	CO	54-16
36645120	Sanders Paul L	IL	

Serial#	Name(Last First Initial)	USA	Camp
34702999	Sasser Gerald E	AL	43-27
17165508	Scarborough Byron A	NE	
O&693411	Schaeffer Gerald L	MT	49-11
O&694803	Scherer John P	MO	
33718736	Schmalbach Arthur Jr	MD	
O&747501	Schmaltz Henry	IL	
33235727	Schmidt Miles P	PA	
O&806355	Schmitz Robert K	TX	
O&753163	Schneider Olin E	OH	
35516378	Schreiber Willard F	OH	
35519327	Schroeder Robert E	OH	
6937647	Schu Matt	MN	
35790966	Schuch Howard E	OH	
15320407	Schwab Edward T Jr	OH	
16087443	Schwemer Louis E	MI	
32270340	Scott Gilbert H	NJ	
14126383	Scott James R	SC	52-17
18202551	Seal Wilburn W	TX	45-21
16008028	Seaquist Robert W	WI	
O&666202	Sears Leland L	CA	
36281369	Seman Leon	WI	
03756809	Semmler Ewald	MN	45-21
32751707	Seningen Harry C	PA	
O&752971	Sergent Jack T	WV	
O&690999	Sermersheim B V	IN	49-11
17126959	Seuferling C E	KS	54-16
12080820	Shaughnessy James	NY	
37171538	Shaver Robert C	CA	54-16
14039312	Shearin William B	X	45-21
12066409	Sheehan William H	NY	
32718197	Sheridan Thomas V	NY	

Serial#	Name(Last First Initial)	USA	Camp
11106053	Sherman Willard M	MA	
35055820	Shestina Edward J	OH	
33562595	Shinham George		45-21
15335331	Shireman Harold E	IN	
14149021	Shive Verne E	NC	
35347128	Signs William J	IN	
6994978	Sikina John J		54-16
32518685	Sildar Alfred H	NY	
12144964	Simmons Allen F	NY	
36614306	Simmons Gerald J	OH	
18191985	Simmons Ova W	OK	45-21
O&673746	Simonson Robert W	ND	
31312829	Sirois Robert J	CT	49-11
20249416	Skrba George Jr	NJ	
37252040	Slavsky Richard A		45-21
38280283	Slayton Leonard E	TX	49-11
15334648	Sleeper Lewis A Jr	IN	
O&768714	Small Delmar C		45-21
O&814999	Smith Arthur L	MI	
33573737	Smith Clair C	PA	
19079845	Smith Gerald D	ND	
18192008	Smith Haskell R	OK	
34644050	Smith Louis G	SC	
O&401249	Smith Walter A Jr	GA	42-23
O&399635	Snaith William G	FL	
35377015	Snodgrass Wilbur D	WV	
12168044	Snyder Charles L	NY	
32077462	Snyder Franklin H	PA	
11093968	Sooy Charles G	MA	
13028316	Souders Harold A Jr	PA	
O&692570	Southworth Gilbert L	DC	

Serial#	Name(Last First Initial)	USA	Camp
16027993	Spears A C Jr	IN	
11037864	Spinney John F	MA	
20761179	Stamatelos Peter D	IA	
O&433599	Stanley Theodore A	CT	
O&686506	Stapp Grady T	FL	
O&696263	Stauffer George E	PA	
O^396173	Staveley Arthur J	NY	
33426036	Stein Robert C	PA	
34260960	Stephens Leon	AL	
18188184	Stephenson Nelson L	TX	
32720605	Stetz Nicholas	NY	
32358869	Steuerer John J	NY	
01703135	Stevens Beryl H	IN	
O&751770	Stiner Theodore J	HI	
36242977	Stoll Clemens W	WI	
O&439092	Stone Robert L	TN	
O&813972	Stout Eugene W	CA	
39263020	Stratton Kenneth E	CA	54-16
18194716	Stringer Charley J P	OK	45-21
17060928	Stringer Glenn E	KS	
O&812188	Struble Rex L	MI	
O&743916	Stuart Griffin C	AR	
20607827	Sullivan Michael J	IL	
O&742221	Summers Lynn N		
O&686508	Sutton Frank T 3rd	VA	48-11
12025551	Swanberry Patrick D	NY	
16146307	Swearingen Paul	IL	
19203126	Swift Orin D	CA	
T&122075	Szymanek Alphonse	WV	
38351804	Tabor Leon R	NM	
39548868	Tanem Vernon P	CA	

Serial#	Name(Last First Initial)	USA	Camp
34209545	Tatum Louis H	FL	
32893557	Tebar John		45-21
O&805876	Temchulla Frank Jr	PA	
37342733	Terry Glenn F	CO	
O&810072	Teune John	IL	
14136617	Thurmond Robert H	TN	
36384298	Thurston George	IL	
32142554	Tierney Peter G		
35411965	Tillman Harold A	OH	
35753651	Tinney Dale C	MD	#07244 AC
O&562219	Tomlinson Frank E	CA	49-11
15131965	Tond George E	OH	
11119850	Tong Robert M	MA	
15105353	Townsend Warren J	IN	
17120224	Traner Donald J	IA	54-16
6937024	Trantham Hugh W		45-21
32507748	Tripaldi Nunzio	NY	
39845471	Triplett Thomas L		45-21
37343960	Trout James H	CO	
15339220	Trucksis Ralph E	OH	
O&802958	Tucker Leo K	CO	
O&661156	Tuten Wilson P	SC	
12192444	Tynan Lawrence J	NY	
16159819	Ukena William	MI	
O&687785	Ullman Victor H	NY	
O&758895	Ulrich Edward D Jr	CA	
	Ullrich Fred J	MN	
34729969	Underwood Clarence	TN	
32456805	Valla John E	NJ	
37494949	Vansickle Edward L	MO	49-11

Serial#	Name(Last First Initial)	USA	Camp
35596792	Veley Robert A	OH	
O&682745	Wade Robert M Jr	VA	
35345820	Wade Russell L	IN	
37461343	Wagner Charles E Jr	NE	
O&684048	Wallick Wilmer S	CA	
O&742803	Walrath Irvin E	OR	
11098594	Walsh David A	MA	
33457194	Walsh David J	PA	54-16
6925034	Walter Billy	X	
32766091	Ward Edward P	NJ	49-11
17063310	Ward John R	ND	
O&761221	Ware James R	CA	
O&796633	Warner Raymond P	X	45-21
14129440	Warren Ernest R	GA	
34056645	Warren Howard C	FL	
36611741	Wawrytko Stanley A	IL	
15354319	Weaver Arthur D	OH	
32549935	Weber Peter G		45-21
O&671716	Weems William Z Jr		45-21
O&659425	Weil Melvin S Jr	AL	
13121243	Weinberger Bernard	VA	54-16
33757364	Welsh Charles C		45-21
O&818257	Werth Willard J		45-21
31266098	Wescott Raymond E	NH	
O&763434	West Donald V		45-21
O&747612	West John F	IL	
O&707465	Weston Frank H	FL	
17066667	Westphal Keith J	KY	
33207473	Wexler Milton A	NY	
O&691022	White Charles E	TX	
O&692982	White Ned C	IA	

Serial#	Name(Last First Initial)	USA	Camp
O&712716	White William C		
O&808919	White William H	CA	45-21
O&700865	Whitesides Charles T	VA	
17161824	Whitsitt Hubert S	IL	
O&758133	Wiggins Arthur J	FL	
14047297	Wilburn Robert C		45-21
19024664	Wilen Arthur E	CA	
O&696293	Wiley Adam	OK	
36585636	Wilk Joseph A	MI	
O&753039	Wilkes Roscoe H	NV	
37344497	Williams John H	NV	
O&808328	Williams John J	IL	
O&737687	Williams Lewis H	NC	
O&668870	Williams Raymond	KY	
O&752731	Williams Richard B	VA	49-11
O&689719	Williams Richard L	MT	
O&703674	Williamson Mervyn	VA	
O&692107	Williamson Robert L	VA	
39123904	Willis Alba W	CA	
O&749993	Winder Keith R	OH	
O&723520	Woll David		45-21
36269546	Woolridge Francis N	WI	
35583129	Wylie Ray F	IN	
O&385447	Yeager William H Jr	TX	45-21
12081262	Yaus William H		45-21
12139207	Yeaton Robert R	NY	
36480088	Young George V		45-21
O&817565	Young Stuart F		45-21
O&809683	Youngclaus George	CO	
O&691076	Yttri Vilas R	WI	
35582786	Yurtanas Joseph B	IN	

Serial#	Name(Last First Initial)	USA	Camp
20631167	Za Zula Theodore	MI	
35409122	Zeger Wilbur M	OH	
39202210	Ziegenfuss John H	PA	
O&752375	Zimmerman John L	OR	

APPENDIX E

AMERICAN POWS WHO DIED AT BUCHAREST
(INCOMPLETE)

SERIAL#	NAME (Last First Initial)	USA	CAMP
35638142	Belcher John W	OH	
36122950	Carpenter Clarence H	MI	
14104597	Burge Arthur P	GA	
06544976	Comfort Donald G (?)	MT	
38411076	DeHart R C	TX	
6900035	Farrington(?) E F		
33051166	Zintak Joseph P	PA	
12134883	Gindes Richard	NJ	
33756798	Harteis Harry G	PA	
693965	Hugo John J (?)		
33605688	Gryniewicki, Richard	PA	
O&716316	Joseph Anthony (?)	NM	
35527757	Keevert Laverne	OH	
O&713205	MacDonald John A	CA	
39207747	Muhoy Elgen K (?)		
892516	Ortego Jossenn J R		

SERIAL#	NAME (Last First Initial)	USA	CAMP
O&690718	Roberts Edward C Jr	PA	
O&804406	Rose Lawrence Z	OH	
693319	Santer James W		
14103043	Schuck Lewis H		
38028212	Silguero Alfredo	TX	
38288091	Stinkler John J		
32477571	Szaras Marion J	NY	
R&273064	Wood G A	DE	

APPENDIX F

AIRFOIL;
WHY IT GENERATES LIFT

Under standard conditions, air pressure at sea level is near 14.2 lbs per square inch, indicating that every square inch of a surface (i.e., the back of one's hand) is under a pressure of 14.2 lbs. Two square inches are under 28.2 lbs of pressure, etc…, the total pressure being the number of square inches multiplied by 14.2 lbs. An airplane wing, at rest, experiences the same total pressure on both the top and bottom surfaces. Therefore, the wing doesn't move—it's static. If the total pressure on top of the wing were to be reduced to the point that it was less than the combined total pressure on the bottom surface plus the weight of the wing, then the wing would have sufficient 'lift' to cause it to rise.

Static (unmoving) air produces greater pressure than moving air by the same principle that a baseball thrown straight against a wall results in greater force on the wall than a baseball thrown at an angle. Therefore, if the air moving across the top surface of a wing could somehow be increased to a sufficiently higher velocity than the air moving across the lower surface of a wing, 'lift' would be generated. This phenomenon was described three centuries ago by Daniel Bernoulli, a mathematician, who found that an increase in velocity of a fluid (i.e., air, water, etc…) across a surface is accompanied by a corresponding decrease in pressure of that fluid on such surface.

Consider a wing whose lower surface is nearly flat and whose top surface is noticeably curved in a convex manner. The distance from the wing's leading (frontal) edge to the trailing edge is greater across the top of the wing (the 'curved' surface) than across the bottom surface of the wing. Therefore, when a wing is moving forward, the air flowing across the top surface must travel further (and faster) around the curved surface than the air flowing across the bottom of the wing (across the flat surface). At some point, as the wing moves faster and faster into the oncoming air, the total air pressure exerted on the upper surface of the wing becomes sufficiently less than the total air pressure exerted on the lower surface so that 'lift' occurs. When the total lbs of air pressure on the lower surface—plus the weight in lbs of the associated vehicle—equals and then exceeds the total lbs of air pressure on the upper surface, flight is achieved.

This is an oversimplification; however, the principle applies.

Conventional aircraft wings employed an 'airfoil' (lift generating design) in which the thickest part of the wing was but a short distance back of the frontal edge. Engineers realized that the airfoil generated turbulence in the process of generating lift and that turbulence resulted in parasitic drag and loss in efficiency. In the case of the P-51, they chose to move the thickest part of the wing further back, almost to the midpoint between the leading and trailing edges, thus producing the laminar flow airfoil that created considerably less turbulence and very little drag. The downside of airplanes having the laminar flow airfoil was that the stall speed (take-off and landing speeds) were quite a bit higher than for those aircraft having the conventional airfoils. All other factors being equal, however, a 'laminar airflow' aircraft would travel faster and consume less fuel than its 'standard airfoil' counterpart.

APPENDIX G

PROPELLER;
WHY IT PRODUCES THRUST

A propeller blade has a cross-section similar to that of a wing—it generates 'lift' toward the front. The front surface of the blade has a greater curvature than rear surface. The propeller generates more 'lift' (forward thrust) as the rpm is increased. However, as tip speed increases—the velocity at which the tip of the blade moves during rotation—and approaches the speed of sound, 'lift' begins to level off and actually become negative; that is, the outer end of the propeller begins to push the plane reversely rather than pull it forward. At the same time, the inside section of the propeller—nearer the hub—continues to pull the plane forward, because this section of the propeller is rotating through the air at a velocity considerably less than the speed of sound. A further increase in propeller rpm sets up vibration that can lead to 'metal fatigue' in both the propeller and the aircraft, resulting in total failure (disintegration of structural components).

The P-51 was designed with a much larger propeller— with respect to its diameter—than conventional fighter planes. The reduction gearbox, affixed to the engine drive shaft, reduced the propeller rpm so that, at a theoretical airspeed of 500 mph, the propeller tip speed approached 90% of the speed of sound when rotating at its optimum design rpm.

Another aspect of a propeller blade is its 'twist.' The greatest amount of twist ('pitch') occurs near the hub and decreases steadily toward the tip. The reason is obvious—the tip travels at the greatest radial velocity and therefore 'slices' through more air than the part nearest the hub.

Propellers are constructed with specific degrees of 'pitch' (angle of 'slice') and are labeled as such. For example, a '6042' *fixed pitch* propeller has a tip-to-tip diameter (length) of '60' inches and a pitch of '42' inches. This particular propeller slices through 42 inches (3.5 ft) of air per rotation. If, for example, this propeller is designed to rotate at 2,400 rpm, its forward thrust should move an aircraft a distance of 8,400 feet (3.5 ft/rotation X 2,400 rpm), or about 1.6 miles in one minute. This would be about 95 mph, a rather standard airspeed for a simple airplane such as a J-3 Piper Cub. The P-51 had a *variable pitch* propeller. That is, the pitch could be changed in flight as needed for obtaining maximum performance.

During take-off and landing—when the aircraft is travelling at lowest airspeed—the pitch is set to minimum. At minimum pitch, the powerplant provides maximum RPM and thrust for low airspeed operation. Lower pitch settings also provide better climb performance. As the aircraft accelerates to higher airspeed, higher pitch settings are applied. High propeller pitch is analogous to 'overdrive' in an automobile. Two types of pitch control options were used in the different aircraft. The P-51 was fitted with a General Electric pitch control system on most models, whereas the B-24 and B-17 bombers utilized engine oil pressure for powering the pitch settings. The oil-pressure system was advantageous for the bombers, because propellers could be moved through a wide range of pitch, including complete feathering (aligning the propeller blades straight into the airstream) in order to achieve minimum drag by eliminating 'wind milling.' This was very important when one or more engines failed during flight.

It has been said, "Necessity is the mother of invention." That being the case, invention, technology, and achievement leaped by quantum jumps as world powers competed—some for global dominance, others for survival. Unfortunately, millions of people perished, including many of America's Finest, in denying the quests of a few ruthless maniacs who would rule the world.

INDEX